THE PROPHET
OF HOPE

THE PROPHET
OF HOPE

~ Studies in Zechariah ~

F. B. Meyer

AMBASSADOR

The Prophet Of Hope

This Edition 1995

All rights reserved

ISBN 1 898787 28 X

AMBASSADOR PRODUCTIONS LTD
Providence House
16 Hillview Avenue,
Belfast, BT5 6JR

PREFACE

THERE are several matters of a critical nature which do not come within the scope of this book; such as the quotations from it in the Gospels, and the difference in style between the earlier and later chapters. These are questions that must be discussed before another audience than that which I address, and by a more competent hand.

It has been my single aim to give the salient features and lessons of each chapter, with the object of alluring the Bible-student to a more searching and careful acquaintance with this Prophet.

Haggai, Zechariah, and Malachi, complete the Old Testament canon—their faces turned towards the sunrise, but conscious that darkness still brooded deep over their contemporaries. They remind one of the crisp breeze that awakes a little before the dawn, and announces its advent, to die down into silence and expectancy till the sun appears.

As one who has found spoil, which he would fain share, the author writes across this prophetic treatise, *Dig here*; and hopes that many will be attracted by Zechariah's holy and eager spirit, through which God spake.

The title of this little book lays stress on one thought which pervades the prophecy of Zechariah. He is pre-eminently the Prophet, as Peter is the Apostle, of Hope.

CONTENTS

STUDIES IN ZECHARIAH

I

THE PERMANENCE OF GOD'S WORDS
(ZECHARIAH i. 1-6)

THE PROPHET Zechariah was born in the latter years of the captivity in Babylon. His name means *one whom Jehovah remembers*. It was evidently a common name among the chosen people, as it is borne by several others in the course of Old Testament story. How good it is to be always sure that God thinks of us—even when we forget or believe not ! He remaineth faithful. "I am poor and needy, yet the Lord thinketh upon *me*. How precious are thy thoughts unto me, O God ! How great is the sum of them ! If I should count them, they are more in number than the sand."

Zechariah came of a priestly family. His grandfather (Iddo) is expressly mentioned as accompanying Zerubbabel, the Prince of Judah, and Joshua, the high priest, back to their desolated country (Ezra ii. 1, 2 ; and Neh. xii. 4). His father, Berechiah, probably died when Zechariah was yet a child, and the boy was reared by the grandfather; he is therefore spoken of as the son of Iddo, and from the earliest his young mind must have been imbued with the traditions and habits of the priestly caste.

The first expedition of exiles, to which we have referred, reached Palestine about twenty years before our story opens. The immense majority of the Jews were too well circumstanced in the wealthy land of their conquerors to be in any hurry to return; and only some fifty thousand souls had risked the dangers of the desert and the privations of the new settlement—but these would comprise, without doubt, the flower of the race for piety and national pride.

The majority of the returned exiles probably betook themselves to their ancestral portions in various parts of the country, only a comparatively small number settling among the charred and blackened ruins of Jerusalem. The book of Lamentations describes, in elegiacs broken with sobs, the condition of the city, as their forefathers had left it seventy years before; and that period of desolation and waste must have still further added to the despair of the situation.

How hath the Lord covered the daughter of Zion with a cloud in his anger!

He hath cast down from heaven unto the earth the beauty of Israel,

And hath not remembered his footstool in the day of his anger.

The Lord hath swallowed up all the habitations of Jacob, and hath not pitied;

He hath thrown down in his wrath the strongholds of the daughter of Judah;

He hath burned up Jacob like a flaming fire;

He hath violently taken away his tabernacle, as it were of a garden;

He hath destroyed his Place of Assembly (Lam. ii.).

Amid these piles of blackened ruins, the handful of impoverished captives settled; and for some time after their arrival were occupied in rearing dwellings for themselves, and in setting up some at least of those religious observances of which for so long they had been necessarily deprived (Ezra iii. 3–6). The foundation of the new Temple was laid shortly afterwards amid shouts of joy, which were overborne by the noise of weeping on the part of those who had seen the first house in its glory—"the ancient men."

It was a fair dawn, but was soon overcast; for the enemies of the returned people set themselves to poison the mind of Artaxerxes (Smerdis), who, being a usurper and a magician, did not feel bound to respect the decree of Cyrus, and ordered the cessation of the work. And it ceased for fifteen years (Ezra iv.). At the end of that time Haggai the prophet, and Zechariah, the son of Iddo, began to stir their fellow-countrymen to resume their neglected toils. The political horizon had undergone a great change in the interval; and there was every reason to hope that Darius, who had headed a successful conspiracy against the usurping Smerdis, and had lately ascended the Persian throne, would be favourable to the purpose of the Jewish exiles, since he was a mono-theist, and zealous for the restoration of pure and spiritual religion. So it afterwards proved (Ezra v., vi., especially 7–12).

But the great difficulty experienced by the prophets was with the Jews themselves. "The time was not come," they said, "the time for the Lord's house to be built." In the meanwhile they were living in ceiled houses, whilst God's house lay waste.

First Haggai spoke. On the first day of the sixth month of the second year of Darius, he pointed to the disasters beneath which the country was groaning, that the dews of heaven were stayed and the earth was unproductive; that a drought lay upon the land and upon the mountains, upon the corn, and wine, and oil, upon men and cattle, and upon all the labour of their hands; that they sowed much and brought in little; ate and had not enough; drank and were not filled; clothed themselves but were not warm; earned wages which were dissipated as though holes were at the bottom of the bag—and urged that all these misfortunes were intended by

God as a remonstrance against their laxity and an incentive to diligence. "Why ?" saith the Lord of hosts. "Because of my house that lieth waste, while ye run, every man to his own house" (Hag. i. 1–11).

"Then Zerubbabel the son of Shealtiel, and Joshua the son of Josedech, the high priest, with all the remnant of the people, obeyed the voice of the Lord their God, and the words of Haggai the prophet, as the Lord their God had sent him, and the people did fear before the Lord. Then spake Haggai, the Lord's messenger, in the Lord's message unto the people, saying, I am with you, saith the Lord. And the Lord stirred up the spirit of Zerubbabel the son of Shealtiel, Governor of Judah, and the spirit of Joshua the son of Josedech, the high priest, and the spirit of all the remnant of the people; and they came and did work in the house of the Lord of Hosts, their God, in the four-and-twentieth day of the sixth month, in the second year of Darius the King" (Hag. i. 12–15).

In the following month, the seventh, a very encouraging word came again through the mouth of Haggai, predicting that the latter glory of the new Temple should even excel that of the former one; a glory not of gold or silver or precious stones, but the spiritual radiance and splendour of Him who was to be the Desire of all nations, and whose advent was destined to invest that building with eternal significance and interest (Hag. ii. 1–9).

The month after, "the Word of the Lord came unto Zechariah." Probably the Word of the Lord is ever circling through the world, as the waves of wireless telegraphy through the air; but there needs an anointed, prepared, and receptive heart to receive and translate the sacred impressions. In the case of the prophets, however, there would be more than this. They spoke as they were moved or borne along by the Holy Spirit. When the apostle speaks of the senses being exercised to discern good and evil, he suggests that to each

sense of the body there is a corresponding one of the soul;
and this, like that, may become more or less acute. Seek
after the quickened, Spirit-touched soul-sense!

> *Be still and strong,*
> *O Man, my Brother! hold thy sobbing breath,*
> *And keep thy soul's large window pure from wrong!*
> *That so, as life's appointment issueth,*
> *Thy vision may be clear to watch along*
> *The sunset consummation-lights of death!*

Zechariah prefaces his prophecies with a very tender
message. True, he does not slur over the sins of the past.
"The Lord hath been sore displeased with your fathers."
The memory of that displeasure was only too recent, the
signs too obvious; but he hastens to accentuate the divine
pitifulness and tender mercy. "Thus saith the Lord of Hosts:
Return unto Me, and I will return unto you." There never
yet was a backslider for whose return the infinite love of God
did not yearn, and after whom it did not send messages like
this. In this the divine love exceeds human love. Even our
Lord could not depict the father of the prodigal sending
messages into the far country, where he sat among the swine;
but this is precisely what God does. Can you not hear the
peal of the silver bells, borne across the valley?—"Return!
return!" And when thou art yet a great way off, the Father
will see thee, and being moved with compassion, will run and
fall on thy neck, and kiss thee much, and reinstate thee where
thou wast at first. He remembers sins no more.

The only fear was lest God should call in vain. "Be ye not
as your fathers, unto whom the former prophets cried; . . .
but they did not hear, nor hearken unto Me, saith the Lord."
Though the chosen people had suffered so terribly, there was
a pitiful possibility of the obstinacy of the former generation
reappearing in this. Each generation insists on trying its own

bitter experiences, unwarned by the experiences of the preceding.

"Your fathers, where are they ?" They were rebellious and sinned, and have passed away under the divine judgments. "And the prophets, do they live for ever ?" But even though the lips that utter the divine Word wax cold in death, the Word itself remains; and it shall have an ever-abiding force. "But my words and my statutes, which I commanded my servants the prophets, did they not overtake your fathers ?" —as a foe overtakes the flying fugitive. So much so as to extort from them a confession of the righteousness of their doom: and they turned and said, "Like as the Lord of Hosts thought to do unto us, according to our ways and according to our doings, so hath He dealt with us."

The conclusion is forcible and clear. The prophet may die, but the divine word remains. Heaven and earth may pass away, but no word of God shall fail. All flesh is as grass, and all the glory thereof as the flower of grass, more transient still; but the Word of the Lord is incorruptible, it liveth and abideth for ever. The fulfilled predictions of the past— whether threatenings like those which befell the Jews, or promises like those realized in the advent of our Lord—all confirm the certainty that "no word from God is void of power." Let us give the more earnest heed then to his invitations, warnings, threatenings, and promises, fashioning the whole course of our lives by them, and ever remembering that they are the asseverations of "the Lord of Hosts."

That title is specially applied to the Divine Being by the three post-exilic prophets. It occurs in this Introduction, five times in six verses. How significant ! Though the Jews had seen the vast hosts of their enemies arrayed against them in battle, or marshalled in their own distant lands, they were assured that their Jehovah had vaster squadrons yet; and that all the powers of nature, all the restless wills of men, all the unseen kingdoms of the dead, and all the principalities and powers of the heaven—the archangels, angels, seraphim and cherubim—stood obedient to his sovereign sway, going, coming, doing this or that, as He chose. Look up, child of God ! thy Father is also the great King, who doeth as He will "in the army of heaven, and among the inhabitants of the earth." "Bless the Lord, all ye his hosts, ye ministers of his, that do his pleasure. Bless the Lord, O my soul !"

B

II

The Myrtle Valley
(Zechariah i. 7–17)

THREE months had passed since the preceding vision, and the month *Sebat* had come, when the trees begin to shoot, and Zechariah says, "I saw by night." What did he see?

If we may be allowed to follow the suggestion of one of the commentaries, we may imagine that not far from the prophet's home there was a green valley, or bottom, filled with graceful myrtle trees, amid which a water-course had its way. Thither he may have been accustomed to resort for prayer, as our Lord retired among the olive trees outside Jerusalem. It is conceivable that ever since the return of the exiles from Babylon he had paced this green glade, pouring out his heart in words like those which were afterwards uttered by the Angel-Intercessor: "O Lord of Hosts, how long wilt Thou not have mercy on Jerusalem and on the cities of Judah, against which Thou hast had indignation these three-score and ten years?" It is pleasant to pray in the open field of nature; the expanse above is suggestive of eternity and unchangeableness, and all the sounds of Nature's varied orchestra, from the rustle of the wind among the leaves to the long-drawn wave-beat on the sand, are marvellously adapted to be an accompaniment to the voice of supplication.

There was a special significance in the presence of the myrtles which grew in humble and fragrant beauty around. The myrtle was a native of Persia and Assyria. Esther's name, Hadassah, meant *myrtle*. It was, therefore, significant of the return of the exiles from the lands of the north; and its humble beauty was an appropriate symbol of the depressed condition of the chosen people, who could no longer be compared to the spreading cedar, or the deeply rooted oak, but were like the myrtle, which, though graceful and evergreen, is nevertheless an inconspicuous and unassuming plant. Many believers are as the myrtle. Their heart is not haughty, nor their eyes lofty; neither do they exercise themselves in great matters, nor in things too wonderful for them. They still themselves, as a child weaned from its mother; and their hope is in the Lord for evermore.

On the night in question, which may have followed a day of unusual exercise of spirit, Zechariah thought that he was in his favourite valley, surrounded by the myrtles; and *behold*, in the midst of them, "a man riding upon a red horse; and behind him" there was a group of companions, mounted on *horses—red, sorrel, and white*. The whole valley seemed alive with these mysterious figures. They had doubtless been there whenever the prophet had paced to and fro, or knelt in intercession; but never before had his eyes been opened to see them. Ah ! how perpetually are our eyes holden, so that we do not perceive the bands of God's marshalled angels, gathered to our succour. The fountain rises from the desert sands, on which our Ishmaels are dying for thirst; but we perceive it not. The mountains are full of horses and chariots of fire; but we tremble as though there were nothing to prevent the enemy making an end of us. The glorious Lord engirds us, as a broad river with its flashing surface might encircle a city; but only to the anointed eye is his defensive presence made manifest.

Naturally the prophet's curiosity was excited, and he sought the significance of the heavenly vision. "Then said I, O my Lord, what are these ?" This inquiry was addressed to a celestial friend and adviser, with whom Zechariah was in constant fellowship. He often alludes to him as "the Angel that talked with me" (9, 14, 19; iv. 1, 4, 5; v. 5, 10; vi. 4). This celestial visitant must be distinguished from "the

Angel of the Lord," referred to in verse 12, and who could be none other than the Angel of the Covenant, our blessed Lord Himself, to whom, also, the riders gave in their reports (10, 11).

It has often been the comforting reflection of individual saints, that their lives were under the direct tutelage and care of guardian angels. Still God gives his angels charge over us to keep us. Still He sends his angel before us, to bring us into the place that He has prepared. Still the interpreting-angel talks with us—or, as Jerome says, *within* us—and says, "I will show thee what these be."

The holy soul, which has its myrtle valley for prayer, and has been accustomed through long years to pour out its intercessions and supplications before God, though it may have been with small response, is the one for whom presently the vail shall drop from the invisible world; and in that rapturous moment the anointed eye will be opened to behold the ministries of God's high angels, as they go to and fro throughout the world on his embassies; whilst the purged ear will become the auditor of their elevated converse as they discuss the affairs of men, and especially of those intercessions with which Christ pleads for his own. "The man that stood among the myrtle trees answered and said, These are they whom the Lord hath sent to walk to and fro through the earth." Then, as the prophet waited and listened, he heard the report which the angel-scouts handed in to headquarters, one in which they agreed with perfect unanimity: "We have walked to and fro through the earth, and, behold, all the earth sitteth still, and is at rest."

It was a time of almost universal peace. The new empire of Cyrus had become securely settled, and beneath the strong rule of his successors there was a grateful cessation of the throes and convulsions which had ushered in the fall of the empire of the Chaldeans.

But to the peace and prosperity of all surrounding countries the condition of the returned remnant presented a notable and strange contrast. If any spot should be verdant and radiant, surely it should be the hill which the Lord had chosen for Himself; and yet it was desolate. This astounding contrast elicited from the Angel of the Covenant an earnest entreaty that God would show Himself strong on behalf of those whom He had brought back from the land of the enemy. "He answered [as though He were speaking to the prophet's thoughts] and said, O Lord of Hosts, how long wilt thou not have mercy on Jerusalem and on the cities of Judah ?"

This is a beautiful glimpse of the intercessions which emanate from our Lord's unchangeable Melchizedek priest-hood. The believer having viewed Him in his Aaronic ministry, by which He put away sin through the sacrifice of Himself, derives great comfort from considering Him as a Priest for ever after the order of Melchizedek; having no beginning of days nor end of life, but abiding a Priest continually, and ever living to make intercession in the heavenly temple for his people. "Simon, Simon, Satan hath desired to have you, that he may sift you as wheat; but I have prayed for thee." What untold benefit accrues to us from his ceaseless and prevalent prayers !

"And the Lord [i.e., the Angel of the Covenant] answered the angel that talked with me with good words and comfort-able words." It was as though the Father had heard and answered the pleadings of the Son, and returned Him an answer, which he passed on to Zechariah's angel-guide; and then the prophet in turn was bidden proclaim them with the urgency and insistence of a cry: "Thus saith the Lord of Hosts: I am jealous for Jerusalem and for Zion with a great jealousy."

More disclosures of God's will followed; that He was dis-pleased with the nations, who had gone beyond his commis-sion; that He had returned to Jerusalem with great mercies;

that the holy house should be built again; that the line of the builder be stretched again over Jerusalem; that the cities of Judah were his cities, which should yet be spread forth in prosperity; that the Lord should yet comfort Zion and choose Jerusalem.

Zechariah awoke; and, behold, it was a dream. But was it not more? Did he not visit that valley at daybreak with new and awful wonder? And did not the people, when they heard what he had seen, and the message which had been communicated to them, pluck up new courage to prosecute their toils? If God was with them, who could stand against them? If angels were encamping round Jerusalem, how inevitable would be her resurrection from encumbering ruin! The return of God to his city meant her return to the beauty that had attracted the wonder and jealousy of the world (Ps. xlviii).

These words may come under the eye of some who have sighed and cried over the desolations of the house of God, whether of the universal Church, or of some beloved sphere of labour, on which they seem to have expended prayers and tears in vain. Have such waited for fifteen years, as Zechariah did? Have they had their myrtle grove of supplication? Have they remained steadfast and unmoved amid universal surrounding declension? If they could hear the good and comfortable words that are being spoken, how glad and thankful they would be! for when men and women pray like this, they do but echo the prayer of the great Intercessor yonder, and their prayer is the sure precursor of the return of God to his heritage with great mercy. Whenever God lays the state of his Church on the hearts of his people, so that they travail in birth for it, a powerful revival of his work is at hand.

Are you, my reader, desolate through the pressure of long-continued sorrow? God's chastenings have been greatly exaggerated by those who have helped forward the affliction.

What was once a busy scene of active service is waste; your home is desolate; your heart sad. Yet, be of good cheer! There is One that ever liveth to intercede. Jesus has graven you upon the palms of his hands. Your sad lot is ever before Him. He will yet talk with you with good words and comfortable ones. "Turn"—they are his own words—"O backsliding children; for I am married unto you, saith the Lord." "I will heal their backsliding, I will love them freely; for mine anger is turned away." "He is able to save them to the uttermost that come unto God by Him, seeing He ever liveth to make intercession for them."

III

The Second Vision
(Zechariah i. 18–21)

THE NEXT vision was full of comfort. The good words and comfortable words of the previous chapter are continued, like the long-drawn-out sweetness of a lullaby.

As the little group of returned exiles looked nervously out on the mighty world-empires, which surrounded and threatened them, they were filled with alarm. How could they cope with them? There were Bishlam, Mithredath, Tabeel, and the rest of their companions, of the nations whom Nebuchadnezzar had settled in Samaria; Rehum the chancellor, and Shimshai the scribe, so ready in their use of the pen to exert influence on the great kings beyond the river, to make the work of temple-building cease; and the reactionary influences at work in the far-distant court, always adverse to the resuscitation of a subdued nation, like the Jews, which had given such proofs of inveterate independence. Beneath the irresistible pressure of these hostile forces the work of temple-building had already ceased for fifteen years, and there was every fear that the new resolve to arise and build would meet with similar opposition and a similar fate. There was singular appropriateness, therefore, in the prophet's vision: "Then lifted I up mine eyes, and saw, and, behold, four horns."

In the language of a pastoral people like the Jews, the horn naturally represents the pride and power of the ravager and oppressor of the flock. The Divine Shepherd is heard from the very horns of the wild oxen (Ps. xxii. 21); and Daniel speaks of the horn which made war with the saints

24

and overcame them, until the Ancient of Days came. The wild fury of man against the people of God is aptly described by the irruption of a herd of tusked boars, by the charge of the rhinoceros, or the rush of the wild ox on a harmless, defenceless flock, which has no power of resistance, but only of flight.

The number *four* reminds us of the cardinal points of the compass, and indicates that, wherever the people turned, there were foes, which were sworn to resist their attempt to renew their national life. On the north, Chaldea, Assyria, and Samaria; on the south, Egypt and Arabia; on the west, Philistia; and on the east, Ammon and Moab. And it is probable that the Spirit of God looked beyond these to the four great Gentile monarchies, which have occupied, and still occupy, the "Times of the Gentiles," and which were represented in the four metals of Daniel's vision, or in the four great beasts, which one after another emerged from the sea.

As yet Babylon and Medo-Persia alone had arisen; Greece and Rome, the latter including the kingdoms of modern Europe, were to come; but all were included in this one comprehensive glance at the kings of the earth, which set themselves, and the rulers who took counsel together, against the Lord and against his Anointed, saying:

Let us break their bands asunder,
And cast away their cords from us.

We must not forget that God Himself gave these world-powers their authority. He says, in Isaiah, "I was wroth with my people; I profaned mine inheritance, and gave them into thine hand" (Isa. xlvii. 6, 7). And in Daniel He lifts the vail and shows that the world-rulers represent not flesh and blood merely, but malign and mighty spirits that actuate and inspire them (Dan. x. 13–20). As long as God's people are perfect in their loyalty and obedience towards Him, they need fear the power of no adversary whatsoever; but when there is a break in the holy connection which binds Him and them in an inviolable safety, it seems as though all the forces of evil are set free to bear down on and ravage them, until their chastisement is completed, and they return to their first love.

If we were asked to name the four horns which are ravaging the Church in the present day, we should not hesitate to say that they are *Priestcraft*, *Worldliness*, *Christian Science*, and *Spiritualism*.

Priestcraft, which substitutes the priest for the living Saviour; rites for faith; and the sacrifice of the Mass for that once offered and finished on the cross; and which is corrupting and undermining, by the accursed system of the confessional, the home-life of our country, as it has that of every nation which has fallen under its blighting scourge.

Worldliness, to which our Lord alludes in his description of the lusts, the strong desires for other things, which enter into competition with the seed sown in our hearts, and make it unfruitful.

Christian Science, which, under the specious use of Christian terms, really eviscerates Christianity of its essential doctrines, making sin an illusion and its penalty a mortal dream; denying the Atonement, and the true nature of Jesus Christ; and teaching men to look on sin, sickness, and death, as matters of wrong thinking rather than wrong being and doing.

Spiritualism, which reduces Christ to the level of a medium, and works lying wonders by the aid of seducing spirits.

As we look on these and kindred evils which are just now invading and ravaging the professing Church, we may well adopt the words of the prophet: "And I said unto the Angel that talked with me, What are these? And he answered me, These are the horns which have scattered Judah, Israel, and Jerusalem."

In every life there are similar experiences. Sometimes, when we lift up our eyes, we find ourselves begirt with opposition and threatened by hostile powers. Think of the martyr-host who have witnessed for God in every age, and who could reiterate the words of the greatest Sufferer of all, "Many bulls have compassed Me, strong bulls of Bashan have beset Me round about; they gape upon Me with their mouth as a ravening and a roaring lion." Ignatius, who complains that his custodians were like "ten leopards, who only wax worse when they are kindly treated"; Blandina, the girl slave; Germanicus, the noble youth; the Waldenses, whose wrongs roused Cromwell's wrath and Milton's muse; the Netherlands, in their long conflict with Philip, when the leaders saw their homes covered again by the ocean from which their ancestors had redeemed them; Madame Guyon, beset by husband, mother-in-law, servants and priests; Samuel Rutherford, and hundreds of his time, harried by the fiercest and most insatiable hate; William Tyndale, the celebrated translator of the English Bible; John G. Paton, beset with savages—these are specimens of a multitude, which no man can number, of every nation, and kindred and people, who have seen the vision of the four horns.

But there is something beyond; and surely it is not without significance that the prophet says: "The Lord showed me four carpenters" (or smiths, R.V.). We have no difficulty in descrying the sources of alarm for ourselves; but we need a Divine Hand to reveal our assured deliverance. "And Elisha prayed and said: Lord, I pray Thee open his eyes, that he may see. And the Lord opened the eyes of the young man and he saw; and, behold, the mountain was full of horses and chariots of fire round about Elisha."

For Babylon, the "carpenter" was Cyrus; for Persia, Alexander; for Greece, the Roman; for Rome, the Gaul. Very different from each other, very ruthless and unsparing; but very well adapted for their work. Commenting on this passage, the late C. H. Spurgeon said: "He who wants to open an oyster must not use a razor; for some works there needs less of daintiness and more of force; Providence does not find clerks, or architects, or gentlemen, to cut off horns, but carpenters. The work needs a man who, when he has work to do, puts his whole strength into it, and beats away with his hammer, or cuts through the wood that lies before him with might and main. Let us not fear for the cause of God; when the horns become too troublesome, the carpenters will be forthcoming to fray them."

Remember how in every age He has found his appropriate messenger. Athanasius frayed Arianism, and Augustine Manichæism; Luther frayed the power of the Pope in Germany, and rough Hugh Latimer in England; Wesley and Whitefield frayed the religious indifference of the last century. When Haldane went to Geneva, he frayed the scepticism which was destroying the Helvetian and Gallic Churches. The Lord knows where to find his servants, and when the predestined hour strikes, there will stand the workman ready. "These are the horns which have scattered Judah, so that no man did lift up his head; but these are come to fray them, to cast down the horns of the nations which lifted up their horn against the land of Judah to scatter it."

O child of God! there have been many horns engaged in scattering thee. Year after year they have wrought sad havoc in thy plans, and cost thee bitter tears. But thine Almighty Friend is greatly displeased that they have hurt thee more than his purposes of chastisement required, and He has resolved that they shall be frayed. He is well able to do this; for He hath sworn that no weapon which is formed against thee shall prosper, and that every tongue which shall rise in judgment against thee shall be condemned. Since the discipline has fulfilled its purpose, it shall be stayed; since the refining fire has purged out the dross, it shall die down; since the winnowing fan has purged the chaff from the wheat, the grain shall no longer be tossed in the breeze. Comfort ye, comfort ye, saith thy God. "For a small moment have I forsaken thee; but with great mercies will I gather thee. In overflowing wrath I hid my face from thee for a moment; but with everlasting kindness will I have mercy on thee, saith the Lord thy Redeemer."

IV

THE MAN WITH THE MEASURING LINE
(ZECHARIAH ii)

A THIRD vision was granted to Zechariah. "I lifted up mine eyes, and saw, and behold a man with a measuring line in his hand."

It was natural enough. We dream of what occupies our waking thoughts; and probably Jerusalem was full of surveyors, engaged in mapping out the new streets and walls.

Some feeble attempts had already been made towards rebuilding; but as yet the ancient sites were principally distinguished by blackened walls and heaps of ruins. The walls of the city, especially, resembled the rubble of a quarry. At last, however, the national pride was awakening the common interest of citizens for their city, of patriots for their fatherland; and the young man with the measuring line in his hand was the fitting embodiment of this new spirit which was breathing throughout the nation.

"Then said I, Whither goest thou? And he said unto me, To measure Jerusalem, to see what is the breadth thereof, and what is the length thereof." It was as though he were defining the limits of the future city, indicating the direction the walls should take, and where they should stay. "Thus far," he kept saying to himself. "The city will never get beyond this boundary line. Grow as it may, it will never exceed this." How apt we are to do this. We are all given to forecasting the future, and place limits, which God has never designed, on the growth of the City of God.

The *Sacramentarian* comes with his measuring line, and insists that Baptism, however administered, and by whomsoever, is the limit; and that all the baptized, Protestants,

Roman Catholics, or of the Greek Church, are included in
God's City; but he refuses to include the member of the
Society of Friends, or the adherent of the Salvation Army.
Slightly modifying the ancient challenge, he says, "Except
ye be baptized, ye cannot be saved."

The *Pessimist* comes with his measuring line, and draws
the plan of the City within the narrowest possible boundaries.
He justifies his forecast by quoting such a text as "Fear not,
little flock"; or "Strait is the gate and narrow is the way that
leadeth unto life, and *few* there be that find it." Sometimes
he fears that he will not enter; at other times he doubts all
others but himself. It may be that depression of spirit, or
long removal from contract with the manifold activities of
God in the world, induce these morbid views—as with Elijah,
who thought that he only was left.

The *Bigot* comes with his measuring line and insists that
the City walls must coincide with his shibboleth, and follow
the tracings of his creed. We have known men much given
to splitting hairs, and making minute and often imaginary
distinctions, who have excommunicated all who did not
exactly agree with them. Very narrow is the enclosure
they mark out for future populations, and very scant their
acreage of the Holy City.

The *Experimentalist* is apt to refuse to consider as Christian
those who have not experienced exactly the same doubts,
fears, ecstasies, deliverances, and cleansings, which he himself has felt. Before a man may be included in his city, he
must have gone through a series of defined and successive
steps or chambers in the divine life.

The *Universalist* goes to the other extreme, and practically
builds his walls around the entire race of man, including
within their circumference every member of the human
family.

It is not for us to fix the boundaries, or insist on our conceptions. These are secret things which belong to the Lord

our God. On the one hand, He only knows if those who call themselves and are considered Christians are really so; and He only can detect the seven thousand who have not bowed the knee to Baal or kissed his image. "Lord," said the apostles on one occasion, "are there few that be saved?" And the Master made answer, as though to turn away their inquiry, "Strive ye to enter in." It is not for us to measure the city, but to be sure that we have entered in.

"Run," said another angel to the prophet's angel-guide, "speak to this young man (*i.e.*, who had the measuring line) saying, Jerusalem shall be inhabited as villages without walls, by reason of the multitude of men and cattle therein." It was useless to mark out boundaries, because the city was destined to exceed all ordinary dimensions, and become so great that no walls would be capable of containing or keeping pace with it. The mighty populations that would congregate at that sacred centre would overflow all limitations, as London has radiated to every point of the compass beyond the narrow enclosure of its ancient walls. It is hard to imagine the time when our own metropolis was contained between London Wall and the Thames.

So shall it be with the saved. We have no right to include in their ranks any who know not God, and obey not the Gospel of our Lord Jesus, who have loved darkness rather than light, because their deeds were evil. But apart from these, there will be a multitude which no man can number, out of every nation and of all tribes, and peoples, and tongues; as stars in the midnight sky, or the sandgrains on the seashore; enough to compensate for the travail of the Redeemer's soul, and to satisfy the yearning love of God. But here an objection might be raised. If the Holy City was to be without walls, would it not be open to every assailant? What would there be to afford a cover for the soldier, or hinder the advance of the spoiler? Supposing that the enemy should say, "I will go up to the land of unwalled villages; I will go to them that are at quiet, that dwell securely, all of them dwelling without walls, and having neither bars nor gates; to take the spoil, and to take the prey" (Ezek. xxxviii. 11)! How then would Israel fare? No sooner is the suggestion made than it is met. "I, saith the Lord, will be unto her a wall of fire round about, and I will be the glory in the midst of her." The image is probably borrowed from the camp-fires with which hunters surround themselves at night to scare off the beasts of prey. Imagine what that means! Just as no pestilence, and certainly no intruder, could break through a cordon of flame, so the unseen but almighty presence of God would be a bulwark on which all the powers of earth and hell would break to their own undoing.

This is what every congregation of believers may perpetually enjoy. They may be situated in the midst of the ancient civilisation of China, or the rude heathenism of West Africa; no walls of wealth, or worldly influence, or prestige may engird them: but they will be absolutely safe, because that cordon of Divine and inviolable protection will enclose them on every side. God will be to them all that walls can be, and more. Indeed, it is better to dwell in an undefended, unwalled city; because we are made more conscious of, and more dependent upon, the environing presence of the Eternal. Surely, the same thought was in the apostle's mind when he gloried and took pleasure in weaknesses, injuries, necessities, persecutions, distresses for Christ's sake; because, when he was weak, then he was strong.

Are you like an unwalled town, with nothing between you and the attacks of poverty, misfortune, godless fellow-work-men, and false brethren? Do not lose heart! you may yet dwell within the devouring fire of God's presence, and be surrounded by the everlasting burnings of his protection (Isa. xxxiii. 14). He hath declared: "No weapon that is formed against thee shall prosper; and every tongue that shall rise in judgment against thee thou shalt condemn."

c

Such an one may well exclaim with David, "I will not be afraid of ten thousands of the people that have set themselves against me round about; for Thou, Lord, art a Shield for me, my glory, and the Lifter up of mine head." Remember to realize God as between you and everything. Some put circumstances between them and God; it is far wiser to put God between oneself and circumstances. Yes, we are as safe, stretched on the bare earth with no covering but the fall of night, as when engirt by massive walls and palace doors. Nay, it is even a blessed thing to be deprived of all that men are so prone to magnify, that we may be thrown back absolutely on God. We never discover how much He can be to the soul until we have no other resource.

Three appeals follow:—*One to the exiles* (verses 6, 7). There were still vast numbers of Jews in Babylon, and to these an earnest invitation was addressed: "Ho, ho, flee from the land of the north, saith the Lord; for I have spread you abroad as the four winds of the heaven, saith the Lord! Ho, Zion, escape thou that dwellest with the daughter of Babylon!" And this invitation was backed by two considerations. On the one hand, safety is assured to them if they return. God would be as quick to protect them as a man to raise his arm when injury is threatened to his eye. On the other hand, they are warned of the certain danger they incur by lingering in Babylon. God was already shaking his hand over that guilty city, as a signal to the nations she had oppressed to gather to her overthrow, and to share her spoils.

Ah, Christian soul, art thou still sojourning in Babylon, conforming to the conventions of the world, moulded by the spirit of the age? Heed the Divine summons to arise and depart. This cannot be thy rest. And flatter not thyself that thou canst do as thy world does, and yet enjoy immunity from its destruction. The conquering troops would make no nice distinctions between Jews and Babylonians, but would slay indiscriminately; and the recoil of natural law, violated by the professing Christian, will be as sharp and inevitable as on those who do not assume to be other than men of the world. Thou mayest be a child of God; but if this do not prevent thee from behaving as a child of this world, it will not prevent thee from suffering as the children of this world suffer when inevitable retribution befalls.

How comforting it is to know that our souls are as safe and dear to God as the apple of his eye ! for there is no part of the body so safely guarded as the eye. The strong frontal bones, the brow or eyelash to intercept the dust, the lid to protect from scorching glare, the sensitive tear-glands incessantly pouring their crystal tides over its surface—what a wealth of delicate machinery for its safety and health ! We have all these in God. He is always on the alert to warn, defend, and cleanse us. "I, the Lord, do keep it; I will water it every moment ! lest any hurt it, I will keep it night and day."

An Appeal to Zion (verse 10). The daughter of Zion might be a scattered remnant, settled amid the blackened ruins of the city; but she might well sing and rejoice, since God declared his willingness to come and share her humble lot, helping her children in their toils, and attracting many nations to Himself. "Lo, I come, and I will dwell in the midst of thee, saith the Lord." She might well dispense with walls and bulwarks, with splendid buildings and holy fanes, since God was in the midst of her. When the tabernacle of God is with men, and He dwells with them, wiping away all tears, there is no mourning nor crying nor pain; but the mouth is filled with laughter, and the tongue with singing. Sometimes the Christian gets a vision of this. He realizes that since God has come into the midst of his work, it is no longer his, but God's; he is only the agent and errand-lad. *God* comforts and teaches the people; *God* restores the ruins; *God* builds the walls of Jerusalem; *God* does good in his good

pleasure to Zion; *God* attracts the people, who join themselves not to a congregation, a church, or a minister, but to
the Lord, and become his. He is not only a wall of fire
round about, but the glory in the midst.

An Appeal to all Flesh (verse 13). In the bold imagery of
Scripture, God is sometimes represented as sleeping (not that
there is any weariness or indifference in the Divine nature,
for He that keeps us neither slumbers nor sleeps, but) to
account for his apparent apathy. Such times are always
those in which Zion herself slumbers in Sleepy Hollow. There
never can be any change in his power or tenderness; but the
exertion of his energy is often arrested through the indifference and unbelief of his people.

When the Church awakes to repentance, humiliation, and
prayer, God is said to awake. The stir among the restored
exiles, in consequence of the preaching of Zechariah and
Haggai, is here described as his awakening—*not, however,
that He had ever slept.*

When God arouses Himself, let all flesh be silent before
Him. Let there be the silence of reverence, of eager expectancy, of humble obedience, of wistful desire. "Be silent, O
all flesh, before the Lord: for He is raised up out of his holy
habitation." "My soul, be silent unto God, for my expecta-
tion is from Him."

V

JOSHUA THE PRIEST
(ZECHARIAH iii.)

WE LEARN from the Book of Ezra (ii. 36-39) that among the exiles who returned with Zerubbabel from Babylon, were Joshua or Jeshua, and 4,289 priests. But they were in a sorry plight—their character is described by the prophet Malachi; and it was in sad contrast, as he suggests, to the original type of the priesthood represented in Phinehas.

They despised God's name. Without scruple they offered on his altar the lame, the blind, and the sick. They said that the table of the Lord was polluted, and the fruit thereof, even his meat, contemptible. They did not hesitate to affirm that the routine of Levitical service was a weariness; and they snuffed at it, and brought that which was taken by violence, or the lame and the sick. They had turned aside out of the way themselves, and had caused many to stumble in the law. From these disgraceful characteristics the prophet turned to paint, with a few bold touches, the noble priest whose burning zeal for the honour of God averted his wrath from the people, and secured for himself and his seed after him the covenant of an everlasting priesthood (Num. xxv. 10-13).

"My covenant was with him," the spirit of God declares, "of life and peace; and I gave them to him that he might fear: and he feared Me, and stood in awe of my name. The law of truth was in his mouth, and unrighteousness was not found in his lips; he walked with Me in peace and uprightness, and did turn many away from iniquity" (Mal. ii. 5, 6).

As a judgment on the priesthood, the whole body had fallen under great reproach: "Therefore have I also made you contemptible and base before all the people, according as ye have not kept my ways" (Mal. ii. 9).

There is every reason to believe, also, that the regulations for the maintenance of the priesthood by the people had fallen into disuse; so that they had neither robes, nor vessels, nor the proper equipment required for the stately ceremonial of the House of God. Under such conditions there was great propriety in Zechariah's vision of Joshua, the high priest, and his fellows that sat before him: "And He showed me Joshua the high priest, standing before the Angel of the Lord. . . . Now Joshua was clothed with filthy garments and stood before the Angel." There was no mitre on his head, no insignia of exalted office on his person; whilst his dishevelled robes told the sad story of neglect. The description at least reflected the general conception entertained of the priesthood; and the question may even have been raised as to whether there was any use in rebuilding the Temple whilst the officiating ministers were so unworthy of their high calling.

There have been times in the past when the leaders of various branches of the professing Church might have been described in similar terms; when the services of God's House have been performed in a slovenly and perfunctory manner; when the religious instincts of the people have been subordinated to the sport, pleasure, and material advantages, of their religious teachers; when services have been without decorum, prayers without reverence, music without taste, buildings in such repair as would not for a moment be tolerated in our homes—everywhere dirt, cobwebs, neglect. Such a condition of things may still be described as the robing of the priestly caste in filthy garments.

But is there not another and deeper meaning in these words? Recall the Angel's words: "Hear now, O Joshua, the high priest, thou and thy fellows that sit before thee; for they are men which are a sign." May not this mean that they represent all who have been made priests unto God, called "to offer up spiritual sacrifices acceptable to God by Jesus Christ"? (1 Pet. ii. 5). Are there not times in our lives when we feel unfit to render that sacred service? It may be at the hour of evening prayer, when the household is assembling; but we hesitate to open the sacred Word, or engage in prayer, because something has gone amiss during the preceding hours, which has soiled the heart and ruffled the inward peace. It may be, as we take our wonted seat in the House of God on the morning of God's day, and there flashes across us the memory of habits indulged, practices sanctioned, methods of making money pursued, which are unworthy of our Christian profession; and again our hearts condemn us. Or, as we ascend the pulpit, take our class, mingle with our fellow workers, we remember outbursts of irritability, proud and vainglorious thoughts, words and deeds of senseless folly; and we feel the incongruity of standing up as God's messengers between the living and the dead. At all such times we are, like Joshua, clothed in filthy garments.

The sense of shame becomes more acute when we stand before the Angel of the Lord. "He showed me Joshua, the high priest, standing before the Angel of the Lord." In the world's twilight much may pass muster which, in the light of that sweet, pure, face, must be utterly condemned. Garments which served us well enough in the short, dark winter days are laid aside when spring arrives; they will not bear the searching scrutiny of the light. In the ordinary life of our homes, we are less particular of our attire than when, on some special occasion, we have to undergo the inspection of stranger eyes. Thus we are prone to compare ourselves with ourselves, or with others, and to argue that the habit of our soul is not specially defiled. Alas! we reason thus in the dark. But when the white light of the throne of God breaks on us, we cry with Job: "If I wash myself with snow-water, and make my hands never so clean, yet wilt Thou plunge me in the ditch, and mine own clothes shall abhor me."

Joshua must have felt much as Isaiah did, when he was passing through the supreme crisis of his life. Prophet though he were, admired and beloved by the good, hated by the bad, when he beheld the Lord sitting on his high and exalted throne, the cry of soul-anguish was extorted from him: "Woe is me, for I am undone." He was probably the last man in Israel who would have been deemed capable of such a confession; yet he was the first to make it. The greatest saints are they who, like Augustine, write confessions. The larger the sphere of light, the wider the circumference of darkness. The more we know of God, the more we loathe ourselves and repent.

What is to be done under such circumstances? Renounce our priesthood? Disclaim its God-given functions? No: remain standing before the Angel. He knows all—we need not shrink from his searching eyes—but He loves infinitely. He has power to make our iniquity pass from us, and clothe us with change of raiment—that white linen which is the righteousness of saints.

It is at such moments, however, that our great adversary puts forth his worst insinuations. "Satan standing at his right hand to be his adversary." Since he was cast out of his first estate, he has been the antagonist of God, the hater of good, and the accuser of the brethren. He discovers the weak spots in character, and thrusts at them; the secret defects of the saints, and proclaims them upon the house-tops; the least symptom of disloyalty, inconstancy, and mixture of motive, and flaunts it before God's angels. He is keen as steel, and cruel as hell. Ah, it is awful to think with what implacability he rages against us !

When we pray, he is quick to detect the wandering thought,

the mechanical repetition of well-worn phrases, the flagging fervour. With a sneer, he says, "Dost thou hear *that* ? Is not this the voice of one whom Thou hast redeemed ?"

When we work for God, he is keen to notice our desire to dazzle our fellows, to secure name and fame, to use the cross as a ladder for our own exaltation instead of our Master's. "Is this," he hisses, "the kind of service which thy chosen servants offer Thee ?"

When we approach the Lord's table, and our hearts are cold in the very presence of that mystery of Love, he claps his hands in glee, and takes care to taunt the Bridegroom with the irresponsiveness and coolness of the Bride. And Christ suffers much. He had noticed all this; but who cares to be accosted with that which is already gnawing at your heart !

And when, like Job, we do bear trial patiently and nobly, the great adversary suggests that we do it from a selfish motive—"Doth Job serve God for nought ?"

Satan cannot reach the Son of God now, save through the members of his Body; but he misses no opportunity of thrusting at *Him*, as he accuses *them*.

Let us now turn to notice the intervention and answer of the Angel of the Covenant. It is spontaneous and unsought. Before Joshua had time to say, "Shelter me," his faithful Friend and Advocate had cast around him the assurance of his protection, and had silenced the adversary. *The Lord rebuke thee, O Satan.* As the Aaronic Priest, He died; but as the Melchizedek Priest, He ever lives to make intercession on our behalf; and as the torpedoes of the enemy are launched against us, He catches them in the net of his Intercession, and makes them powerless to hurt. Before we call, He answers. Before we realize the strong and cunning charges accumulated against us, He has rebutted them. In the same breath in which the Master told Peter that Satan had sought to sift him as wheat, He told him that He had prayed for him.

It is founded on electing grace. For He says: "The Lord that hath chosen Jerusalem rebuke thee." Before ever He chose her, He must have foreseen all that she would become, her backslidings and rebellions, her filthy garments, her wounds and bruises and putrefying sores; but, notwithstanding all, He set his heart upon her. Surely, then, He would not abandon her because of anything that her adversary might rake up to her discredit. He knew the worst about her before He chose her as his own; nothing could happen that had not been well considered in the white light of eternity. Satan could allege nothing which the Advocate had not weighed in the balances of his Divine prescience. He had realized the very worst before making his final choice.

These are foundation thoughts, on which we rest the structure of our hopes. When we are most agonized at the memory of recent failure, most distressed as we weigh and consider the cruelty and meanness of our selfish actions, most ashamed for the vileness and inveteracy of our impure and unholy passions, we can only turn to those passages which assure us that we were chosen in Christ before the foundation of the world and that He predestinated those whom He foreknew. For God to reject us now would be a reflection on his omnipotence. Yes, thou great adversary thou canst not tell our Lord worse things about us than He knows; and notwithstanding all. He loves, and will love.

Moreover, it has already done too much to go back. The point of the metaphor which follows is very reassuring. "Is not this a brand plucked out of the fire?" You have been writing all the morning at your desk, answering letters, assorting papers and manuscripts, destroying much that there was no need to keep. After two or three hours of work, there is a heap of papers which you wish to destroy, and you place them in your stove or fireplace, the fire kindles on them, and they begin to blaze. Suddenly, to your dismay, you remember that there was a cheque or note amongst them, or a letter with an address, or a paper which has cost you hours of work. As quick as thought you rush to the kindling flames, and snatch away the paper, and attempt to stay the gnawing edge of flame. But what an appearance the paper suggests ! It is yellow with smoke, charred and brittle round the edges, scorched and hot, here and there are gaps—it is a brand plucked out of the fire. Would you have snatched it out if you had not valued it ? And, after you have taken such pains to rescue it, is it likely that you would thrust it back to destruction ? And would Jehovah have snatched Israel out of Babylon, and expended so much time and care over her, if at the end He meant to destroy her ? The fact of his having done so much, not only proved his love, but implied its continuance.

What depths of consolation are here ! As we look back on our lives, we become aware of the narrowness of our escape from dangers which overwhelmed others. We have been involved in companionships and practices which have ruined others irretrievably; but somehow, though we are charred and blackened, we have escaped the ultimate results. We have been plucked out of the burning. What can we infer from so gracious an interposition, except that we have been preserved for some high and useful purpose; and that God will yet make use of us for his kingdom and glory, in spite of all that Satan may say or do on the other side—and this because He sees, what Satan cannot see, the bitterness of our repentance, the poignancy of our grief, and the sincere desire of our hearts yet to serve Him, before we go hence.

Manoah's wife was perfectly justified in meeting the fears of her timorous husband by saying, "If the Lord were pleased to kill us, He would not have told us such things as these." All the past is an argument for faith. God resembles an investor who has sunk so much in an undertaking that, though it has hitherto proved unprofitable, he dare not abandon it; he is bound to go on until the scale turns, and it begins to pay—then he will be abundantly recouped. Has God snatched you from destruction, from the jaws of the lion, and the mouth of hell? It is a proof that He will perfect what concerneth you. Let Satan try his worst, God cannot deny Himself. He does not say, Yea, yea; nay, nay. "Whom He called, them He also justified; and whom He justified, them He also glorified. What then shall we say to these things? If God be for us, who can be against us!"

VI

THE CANDLESTICK
(ZECHARIAH iv)

ON THEIR return from Babylon the Jews were confronted with immense difficulties arising from the opposition of their neighbours, their want of resources, and the incompetence of their leaders. The last was probably their most serious difficulty. Joshua was clothed with filthy garments, and Zerubbabel had faltered in his attempt to rear the Temple. His hands had laid the foundation, but, after a brief effort, they had fallen paralysed by his side. Royal blood was in his veins, but he sadly lacked the energy and faith of the princes of his line. The rebuilding of the Temple had been greatly hindered, and for some years had been entirely suspended; and, all around, the heaped-up ruins and unused materials showed how much needed to be done. The suspicion may have suggested itself, and spread from lip to lip, that there could be no improvement, no hope of advance, whilst Zerubbabel was to lead.

These difficulties and forebodings rose like a mountain range between the returned exiles and the accomplishment of their purpose. Not more absolutely do the Himalayas, which seem like a vision of clouds to dwellers on the plains of India, wall out invasions and bar the northern route, than did these tremendous obstacles rear themselves before the returned remnant.

It was at this juncture, and to reassure them, that the angel that talked with Zechariah came again, and waked him, as a man that is wakened out of his sleep. He did not minimise the greatness of the discouragements, but he brought a message of hope. Even though Zerubbabel might lack the essentials of a great leader, yet the success of their undertaking did not depend upon him, but on the Divine power, which was working through him to achieve the Divine purpose. "Then he answered and spake unto me, saying, This is the word of the Lord unto Zerubbabel, saying, Not by might, nor by power, but by my Spirit, saith the Lord of Hosts. Who art thou, O great mountain ? Before Zerubbabel thou shalt become a plain : and he shall bring forth the head-stone with shoutings of Grace, grace unto it."

In the most express and unmistakable terms Zechariah was further assured that God would certainly fulfil his word through this scion of David's house. "Moreover, the word of the Lord came unto me, saying, The hands of Zerubbabel have laid the foundations of this house; his hands shall also finish it." With what new pleasure the prophet would contemplate the state of the Temple area; and, the day of small things, as it undoubtedly was ! With what new fortitude he would bear the adverse criticisms of the old men who had seen the glory of the former house, and were loth to believe that anything could come of beginning so feeble and delayed! He could already see the Prince of Judah, standing in the sunny air, plummet and trowel in hand, fixing the capstone in its place, amid the enthusiastic shouts of the people. Better than all, he could see the eyes of God, seven in number, because of their perfection, which run to and fro throughout the whole earth, rejoicing as they beheld the plummet in his hand. We pause here for a moment to absorb the sweetness of the suggestion, that God delights in his people's work for Him, and joins his congratulations with theirs when the crown is placed on their labours.

In order to make God's meaning clearer, the prophet was granted the vision of the candlestick (lamp-stand), the gist of which was that the wick, though necessary to the light, played a very inconsiderable part in its production. It had no illuminating power; it could only smoke, and char, and smoulder. At the best, it could only be a medium between the oil in the cistern and the fire that burnt on its serried edge. Thus Zerubbabel might be weak and flexible as a wick, but none of his deficiencies could hinder him finishing the work to which he had been called, if only his spirit was kindled with the Divine fire, and fed continually by the gracious influences of the Holy Spirit.

The candlestick, which Zechariah beheld in prophetic ecstasy, was evidently fashioned on the model of that in the Temple, the shape of which is still preserved to us on the Arch of Titus. At the top there was a large bowl or cistern filled with the golden oil, in which the wicks of the lamps were dipped, and which stole up their texture to burn for the light of all that were in the house. The branches radiated from a central stem to the seven lamps. According to the R.V., there were seven pipes to each lamp, and therefore forty-nine in all. Nor was this all. On either side of this massive candlestick stood an olive-tree, from the heart of which, by a golden pipe, the oil was continually being poured into the reservoir; so that even though it might be limited in its containing power, there could be no failure in its ability to meet the incessant demands of its lamps.

So far as the Jews were concerned, the meaning of the vision was obvious. They were represented in the candlestick, of which the many lamps and the precious metal of its composition set forth their perfection and preciousness in the thought of God. Their function was to shed the light of his knowledge on the world, as it lay under the power of darkness; whilst, to aid them in fulfilling this mission, Divine supplies would be forthcoming from a celestial and living source, and brought to them through the golden pipes, of which one represented Joshua the priest, and the other Zerubbabel the prince. These men, therefore, were but mediums for Divine communications. Their sufficiency was not of themselves, but of God. The mission of Israel would be realized not by them, but by the Spirit of God through them. They might seem altogether helpless and inadequate; but a living fountain of oil was prepared to furnish them with inexhaustible supplies.

For us, too, this vision is full of teaching, encouragement, and admonition, to which we would do well if we pay heed.

The first chapter of the Book of Revelation, which compares the work of the Church during the present age to seven light-bringing candlesticks, suggests the application of this vision of Zechariah's to ourselves. As yet dawn has not broken; darkness envelops the earth, and gross darkness the peoples. But God has called his people, in the meanwhile, to "shine as lights in the world, holding forth the word of life." Let us recognise the important work to which God has called us; and whether it be as the household candle, the street lamp, or the gleam of the lighthouse, let us beware of hiding our light under a bushel, lest men stumble to their destruction. The lights of a dark night seldom receive their meed of notice or gratitude; but how could we do without them? And though the children of this world rarely recognise their indebtedness to the Christian Church, they would be in a sorry plight if it were not for its three-fold beam of faith, hope, and love.

The golden bowl filled with oil is an eloquent symbol of the relationship of our Redeemer to his people. "It hath pleased the Father that in Him should all fulness dwell." The fulness of the Holy Spirit is always at high-water mark within his glorious nature. It is not possible to imagine any aspect of Holy Ghost fulness which is not embraced and included in our glorious Lord; and there is no quality needed for the outshining of Christian character which is not richly stored in Him; He is "the fulness of the God-head bodily." His the spirit of wisdom and understanding; his the spirit of counsel and might; his the spirit of understanding and of the fear of the Lord; and He "is made unto us wisdom, and righteousness, and sanctification, and redemption." Press this thought to your heart, child of God, and dwell on it— that in Christ are hidden all the treasures of wisdom and knowledge; He is the ocean-basin of God's infinite resources, that we may for ever draw on his stores, and be replenished from his fulness with grace upon grace.

It was explained to Zechariah that the olive trees on either side of the candlestick were *the two sons of oil that stand by the Lord of the whole earth*. If, in its primary significance, this figure indicated the royal and priestly elements of the Jewish national life, in our case it signifies the royal priest-hood of our Lord and of us his people. He is a Priest upon his throne. He is a Priest for ever after the order of Melchizedek who was King of Salem as well as Priest of the Most High God. Had He been only our Aaron, He would have made peace between God and us by the shedding of blood, and have gone into the Holy of Holies to intercede; but the vail would have fallen intact behind Him, and He would have had no power to introduce us into the Most Holy Place, and maintain us there. He would not have been able to com-municate a royal and victorious life, which defies the power of sin, and goes forth to conquer in eternal vigour and beauty. Christ is King as well as Priest; and therefore He not only brings us nigh to God, but makes us sit with Him in the heavenlies of his eternal supremacy.

Yes, friend, we may be but as wicks, with no pith or power of our own, smoking, charring, burning out; unnoticed amid the flame we yield; unrewarded and unthanked; pieces of coarse tow. But let us keep saturated in the fulness that is in Christ Jesus; let us abide in Him; let us dip deep into the well of his supplies—so shall the quality of his glorious nature yield itself up through us to the illumination of men.

It is easy to see what comfort this vision brought to the handful of exiles amid those blackened ruins. It seemed as

D

though mountain ranges of difficulty stood between them and the accomplishment of their great undertaking. But now they learnt that at the best they were only the channels and instruments; and that God was prepared to accomplish the results they sought. It was not to be by their might, nor power, but by his Spirit, pouring into and through them with inexhaustible fulness—as the oil poured into and through the golden pipes from the two olive trees.

We are often menaced by apparently insurmountable difficulties, which extort from us the groan, "O great mountain !" At other times we are oppressed with a sense of our impotence, and of the weight and weariness of life. How can we be always good? How obey the heavenly vision? How last? We are told that Daniel *continued* unto the first year of Cyrus. Ah, this patient endurance and continuance in well-doing ! If we are to live for twenty, thirty, or fifty years from now, in a world in which the shocks, perils, and demands will certainly not diminish as the coming of the Bridegroom draws nigh, shall we be able to endure to the end? Will not the lamp expire before the gust which shall precede the grey dawn of Advent? The outward man decays; will the inward man be always renewed?

These thoughts attracted me to a conversation with the wick of my lamp. For long it had served my purpose, silently ministering as I read beside it. I felt ashamed that I had not before noticed its unobtrusive ministry. I said to the wick :—

"For the service of many months I thank thee."

"What have I done for thee ?"

"Hast thou not given light upon my page ?"

"Indeed, no ; I have no light to give, in proof whereof take me from my bath of oil, and see how quickly I expire. Thou wilt soon turn from me, as a piece of smoking tow. It is not I that burn, but the oil with which my texture is saturated. It is this that lights thee. As for me, I simply mediate between the oil in the cistern and the fire on my edge. See this blackened edge. It slowly decays, but the light continually burns."

"Dost thou never fear becoming exhausted? See how many inches of coil remain! Wilt thou be able to give light till every inch of this is slowly charred and cut away?"

"I have no fear so long as the supply of oil does not fail, if only some kindly hand will remove, from time to time, the charred margin, trimming me, and exposing a fresh edge to the flame. This is my two-fold need: oil and trimming. Give me these, and I shall burn to the end."

"I thank thee, gentle teacher," I said, as I turned away; "thou hast greatly encouraged me. I, too, shall endure, so long as I abide in Him, in whom God has stored the measureless residue of the Spirit; and so long also as the Divine hand, with delicate thoughtfulness, uses the golden snuffers, removing the *débris* and decay, pruning that I may bear fruit; piercing to the dividing asunder of soul and spirit, that I may enter into his rest."

Some among us appear to think that the soul can accumulate a stock of grace, in a sacrament, a convention, or a night of prayer. But this is at variance with the teaching of the wick. It accumulates nothing. It has no stores. From hour to hour it is always on the edge of bankruptcy, but always supplied. So should we live—at every moment giving all we have, but never doubting about the supplies of the future. Bear pain for one moment at a time; there is patience enough in Jesus for the next moment. Do your Christian work with as much energy as though each service were your last. You cannot exhaust God; and your work is to be, not in your might or power, but by his Spirit.

Moment by moment I'm kept in his love;
Moment by moment, I've life from above:
Looking to Jesus! till glory doth shine,
Moment by Moment, O Lord, I am thine.

There is also a warning for us all implied in this vision, to which we must give heed. We must very carefully abide in Christ, that He may abide in us; always recognising his royalty, which calls for obedience; always resting upon his priesthood, which reconciles us to God. In obedience and faith the bond of fellowship is perpetually maintained and strengthened. Every time we do as our Prince bids, though it contradict the strongest desires of our nature; every time we resort to our Priest—there is an accentuation of that fellowship which draws his nature into ours.

Forgive me if I return to this thought again and again. It has become so precious an emblem of my relationship with my Lord, to think of the union between the wick and the limitless supplies of the olive tree. Hour after hour the oil climbs up the wick to the flame: and thus insensibly the grace of the risen Lord passes through the medium of our faith into the radiant beauty of a life on fire with God. O fire of God, thou shalt burn on us for evermore; and our spirits shall be thy candles, because we have learnt to be strengthened with might by his spirit in the inner man, and Christ dwells in our hearts by faith.

We must expect that Christ will use his golden snuffers. Let us not flinch from them. When He seems sacrificing some vital, necessary part of our nature, He is only cutting away the black, charred, burnt-out *débris*. Trust Him. That piece which He has cut away was smoking badly, and spoiling the testimony of the rest. It was better for it to come off; but He thinks so much of this work, that He will use only *golden* snuffers. Can you not trust the hand that holds them? It bears the nail-print of Calvary.

Beware, also, that nothing chokes the golden pipes of obedience to his kingliness, and trust in his priesthood; else the entrance of the golden oil will be arrested. They may soon become stopped by neglect, inattention, or disuse.

Do not weary of the slow advance of your life to Christian

perfection. This is the day of small things; of the foundation-trench rather than the top-stone; of the testing of line and plummet, rather than of shoutings of "Grace, grace unto it." But be of good cheer; the seven eyes of the Lord are upon the worker and the work. They run to and fro throughout the whole earth; but they return to rest in loving interest on the progress of his work. He will perfect that which concerneth you; He cannot forsake the work of his own hands.

Grace all the work shall crown
Through everlasting days;
It lays in Heaven the topmost stone,
And well deserves the praise.

VII

Goings Forth
(Zechariah v, vi. 1–8)

THERE is a clear connection between the three next visions, furnished by the words, *Going forth.* "The curse goes forth over the face of the whole land" (v. 3); "The ephah goeth forth" (v. 6); "The chariots go forth" (vi. 1–5). It is as though Zechariah were permitted to stand in the centre of things, where God is, and was able to see the successive issues of the Divine Providence in respect of the moral government of his people and the world.

I. THE VISION OF THE FLYING ROLL.—The prophet beheld in vision a huge sheet of paper, or dressed skin, prepared for writing, slowly floating in mid-heaven. It seemed to be hovering, and prepared to pounce, as a bird of prey may often be seen on the point of settling over a ploughed field. Its considerable extent, thirty feet by fifteen—the dimensions of the Temple porch—was covered on each side by the solemn curses of the law; on this, by those that condemn the thief; on that, by those condemning the false swearer.

We have already learnt that God had returned to Jerusalem, prepared to become a wall of fire round about, and its glory in the midst; the Temple should be rebuilt, and the priesthood reconstituted; but the people must be made to understand what a solemn thing it was to have God in such near proximity. If He was ready to defend them against their foes, He was also determined to purge out from among them those who transgressed his holy law.

It is clear that this young community was specially cursed by these twin sins. Men were fraudulent and mendacious. They got the better of their customers if they had the chance; and then, with unblushing effrontery, lied to conceal their frauds. These are always the sins of a mercantile community; and they are as prevalent in London and New York, in Bombay and Melbourne, as ever they were in the newly restored Jerusalem. But God is always pledged to deal with them, in the interests of society itself, which must be undermined if they be allowed to prevail unchecked. Over the great commercial centres of the world—yes, and over the great emporiums of trade—that roll still hangs, and the curse of God threatens to fall.

The effect of the curse is told in graphic symbolism. It seemed after a time to settle down on certain houses. They may have been respectable houses, the houses of men that were held in reverent repute, houses which were often alight with the lamps of high festival; but by the settling down of that roll, the master of such and such a house was indicated as being either a thief or a liar. "I will cause it to go forth, saith the Lord of Hosts, and it shall enter into the house of the thief, and into the house of him that sweareth falsely by my name."

That, however, was not the end, either of the vision or of those divine dealings which the vision describes. The interpreting angel goes on to say: "It shall abide in the midst of his house, and shall consume it, with the timber thereof, and the stones thereof." It was as though, from the moment that the curse settled down, the whole fabric of the house commenced to rot; and the owner might fairly adopt the words of Leviticus: "There seemeth to me to be, as it were, a plague in the house."

How terribly those words have been fulfilled in the case of people and families we have known ! It has seemed as though there were a plague in the house. The fortune which had been accumulated with such toil has crumbled; the children turned out sources of heartrending grief; the reputation of the father has become irretrievably tarnished. "There is a plague spread in the house; it is a fretting leprosy, it is unclean." No man can stand against that curse. It confronts him everywhere. It touches his most substantial effects, and they pulverize, as furniture eaten through by white ants. It is as though he were condemned to hear, like another Job, the voices of successive messengers, announcing that they only are left to tell the story of irremediable disaster. Timber and stones, however carved and chiselled, crumble to ash and dust ! How awfully realistic ! How terribly true !

II. THE VISION OF THE EPHAH.—Again the prophet's eyes were directed by the angel that spoke with him towards midheaven, and he saw a yet more graphic symbol. An ephah was seen careering through the air. "I said, What is it ? And he said, This is the ephah that goeth forth. He said, moreover, This is their resemblance in all the land." As much as to say that the Jews were known throughout the world of that time as traders, who were constantly handling the Hebrew dry measure, containing about a bushel, or seven-and-a-half gallons.

Presently the cover was lifted off, and a woman was seen sitting in the midst of the ephah. "And he said, This is Wickedness; and he cast her down into the midst of the ephah: and he cast the weight of lead upon the mouth thereof." Does not this clearly mean that the commercial life of these Jewish traders was deeply saturated with wicked practices, and that there was a kind of alliance between them and the impalpable spirit of Wickedness, as illustrated by this personification of evil ?

How often when men slam to the doors of their safes, shut their ledgers, and lock their counting-houses, they seem to place the leaden weight on the top of the ephah containing

wickedness ! They wish to hide it from the eyes of their
nearest and dearest. They would like to hide it from the face
of God Himself.

It is at this juncture, however, that an entirely new turn
is given to this vision. "Then lifted I up mine eyes, and saw,
and behold, there came forth two women, and the wind
was in their wings; now they had wings like the wings of a
stork; and they lifted up the ephah between the earth and
the heaven." The stork has long and wide wings. It is also
a migratory bird. It would have no difficulty in covering the
distance between Jerusalem and Babylon. And, therefore,
storks' wings are attributed to these two women. As two
anointed ones stand by the Lord as his ministers, so these two
women execute his purposes in removing wickedness which
answers to the mystery of iniquity, of which the apostle
speaks.

"Then said I to the angel that talked with me, Whither
do these bear the ephah ? And he said unto me, To build her
an house in the land of Shinar; and when it is prepared, she
shall be set there in her own place." Babylon was far away,
the seat of apostasy from God and demon-worship. It was
meet that Wickedness should be borne thither. But how great
the deliverance for the chosen land !

What comfort is here ! Wickedness may be strongly en-
trenched; but she shall be removed, when once God arises
on the behalf of his people. Do you sigh and cry against it ?
Do you desire that some terrible form of it, which has cursed
your life too long, and alienated the Divine favour, should
be eliminated ? Be encouraged by this vision ! Lift up your
eyes, and see the swift stork-like wings, with the favouring
breeze bearing them forward as they speed to perform God's
behest. If only you are willing, God will certainly free and
deliver you.

Thousands have experienced this deliverance from certain
forms of besetting sin, which have dropped off as the viper

from Paul's hand, as they have received the more perfect
indwelling of the Holy Ghost. Not long after his conversion,
the saintly Fletcher passed into this experience, trod sin
under his feet, and proclaimed that we must not be content
till we have been delivered from the power of sin, through
the indwelling of the Divine Spirit. And Wesley says of
Halyburton: "This great servant of God sometimes fell back,
from the glorious liberty he had received, into the spirit of
fear, and sin, and bondage. But why? Because he did not
abide in Christ; because he did not cleave to Him with all
his heart; because he grieved the Holy Spirit by whom
freedom from sin is rendered the common privilege of all."
From which we infer that Wesley held and taught, that we
are delivered from the power of sin and darkness, just in so
far as we abide in Him who is the light of life. Abide in Him,
and you, too, shall see wickedness borne out of the practical
experience of your life.

III. THE VISION OF THE CHARIOTS.—This is a vision of
Protection and Deliverance. Four chariots are seen issuing
from the mountains that were round about Jerusalem. In
each case the colour of the horses represented the commission
that their hurrying drivers bore to the different nations,
which, before that time, had ravaged the Jewish people.
"Then I answered and said unto the angel that talked with
me: What are these, my lord? And the angel answered and
said unto me: These are the four spirits of Heaven, which
go forth from standing before the Lord of all the earth."

Against the north country, where Babylon lay, two
chariots went forth; whereof the black horses represented
defeat and despair, while the white stood for the victorious
successes of some conquering people, before whom Babylon
would be laid low in the dust—a prediction which was
probably fulfilled in the rise of the third great world-wide
kingdom of Greece, under Alexander the Great.

The grizzled, or piebald, went forth toward the south country, and represent the mixed experiences—partly of disaster, and partly of prosperity—which would befall Egypt, on the southern frontier of the Holy Land. For the word *bay*, the margin suggests the possible alternative *strong*; and this is probably the right rendering. So this one chariot seems to have been allocated to the work of going to and fro in the earth, on a general mission of patrol and defence. If Satan goes to and fro, seeking whom he may injure, the chariots of God go to and fro, to bring succour and deliverance to the saints.

How comforting this vision was and is ! It clearly teaches that, when sin is put away, as between God and his people, He constitutes Himself their gracious Keeper: no weapon that is turned against them prospers, and every tongue that rises in judgment against them is condemned. Woe be to their enemies ! God's Spirit is, in strong metaphor, described as being quited by their overthrow; whilst his chosen dwell always within the precincts of his Almighty guardianship. "They shall dwell securely in the wilderness, and sleep in the woods."

VIII

CHRIST—PRIEST AND KING
(ZECHARIAH vi. 9–15)

AT THIS point an interesting episode breaks in on this wonderful series of visions. From far-off Babylon, where the majority of the Jewish nation was still residing, a deputation of three Jews came to Jerusalem, bringing a present of gold and silver. This donation was evidently intended to aid the little band of returned exiles in their heroic work. Alas, it is still the way in which too many Christians do the work of God! They shrink from personal service; but are quite ready, in lieu of it, to give a subscription in aid of those who are sacrificing ease and emolument that they may give priceless personal service.

The men who brought the gift were Heldai (called Helem in verse 14), Tobijah, and Jedaiah; and they were received and entertained by Josiah, or Hen, the son of Zephaniah.

Zechariah was directed to take the gold and silver, and make a crown (or crowns). These, on some public occasion, and with, perhaps, some little ceremony, were placed on the fair mitre, which, we have already seen, had been set on the high priest's head.

It was a much more significant act than this bare recital of it suggests. These two offices, the sacerdotal and the regal, had been always kept jealously apart in Israel; and when King Uzziah had attempted to burn incense upon the altar of incense, the altercation which ensued in the holy place between himself and the priests, countersigned as their

horror and indignation were by the rising of the brand of
leprosy on his forehand, proved how stringent that separation was. But here the divinely commissioned prophet, by
an unmistakable symbolic act, combined the two offices in
the same individual. And, using a well-understood name
for the Messiah, went on to say: "Thus speaketh the Lord of
Hosts, saying: Behold, the Man whose name is THE BRANCH.
He shall grow up out of his place (*i.e.*, shall emerge from the
obscurity of his early beginnings), and He shall build the
Temple of the Lord; and He shall bear the glory, and shall
sit and rule upon his throne; and He shall be a priest upon
his throne, and the counsel of peace shall be between them
both" (*i.e.*, between these two offices, the priestly and the
regal).

I. NOTICE THIS SIGNIFICANT DESIGNATION OF THE LORD
JESUS—"The Branch." The family of David was like a
decayed tree, the stump of which alone remains; but from
so lowly and unlikely an origin, a shoot or scion would
emanate, which would again become a noble forest tree, and
perpetuate the memory and influence of the royal line. This
imagery is familiar to more than one of the prophets, and, in
every case, can only be applied to "Jesus Christ, the son of
David, the son of Abraham" (Matt. i. 1). "There shall come
forth," says Isaiah, "a shoot out of the stock of Jesse; and a
Branch out of his roots shall bear fruit, and the Spirit of the
Lord shall rest upon Him. In that day shall the Branch of
the Lord be beautiful and glorious." "Behold"—they are
the words of Jeremiah—"the days come, saith the Lord, that
I will raise unto David a righteous Branch, and He shall
reign as King." It is suggested that, in the song of Zacharias,
so full of the glad realization of the fulfilled past, Branch may
be substituted for Dayspring, and he may, therefore, have
quoted this very phrase and said, "The *Branch* from on high
hath visited us" (Luke i. 78).

Certainly David's race had reached a low ebb when Joseph went up from Galilee, out of the city of Nazareth into Judea, to the city of David which is called Bethlehem to be enrolled with Mary his espoused wife, because they were of the house and lineage of David. There was no room for them in the village inn; the new-born Babe was wrapped in swaddling clothes and laid in a manger; and the couple were so straitened for means, that they could only afford to purchase two young pigeons, the gift of the poor, for the mother's thank-offering in the Temple. From that stock, however, the scion has grown into a noble tree, whose branches reach out to the ends of the earth, and whose fruit gives life and blessing to all mankind.

Through a branch the fulness of the root is carried to the fruit, which swells in ruddy beauty on its extremity, and presently falls into the hand of the wayfarer: so Jesus is the blessed channel of communication between the fulness of God and the thirsty wastes of human need. We sit under his shadow with great delight, and his fruit is sweet to our taste.

II. THE COMBINATION IN CHRIST OF THE PRIESTLY AND KINGLY OFFICES.—"He shall be a priest upon his throne." Man's nature demands a PRIEST. Conscious of sin and defilement, he rears an altar wherever he pitches his tent; and, selecting one of his fellows, he separates him from the ordinary duties of life, and bids him stand as mediator and priest between God and himself. It was true thus that Micah addressed the young man, the Levite of Bethlehem-Judah, when he said, "Dwell with me, and be unto me a father and priest; and I will give thee ten pieces of silver by the year, and thine apparel, and thy victuals."

If an argument were needed to prove the unity of the human family, it surely would be suggested by the universal distribution of temples and altars over the world, as though

men were everywhere alike in this—that they know themselves to be sinful, and desire to find some way of propitiating
and approaching the Almighty.

In the Levitical system, and, above all, in Jesus Christ, God
has met this universal craving of the human heart. Indeed,
no religion is destined to universal supremacy that does not
provide for the consciousness of guilt, and reveal a merciful
and faithful priest, appointed in things pertaining to God,
that he may offer both gifts and sacrifices for sins, and bear
gently with the ignorant and erring.

Man also requires A KING. God had designed to meet this
need by Himself being Israel's King, that they should *not*
be "like other nations," but a peculiar people unto Him.
They were following natural promptings, when the Israelites
came to Samuel and said: "We will have a king over us, that
we also may be like the other nations, and that our king may
judge us, and go out before us, and fight our battles." Man
needs a leader—one whom he may admire and obey; from
whom he may receive indisputable commands; and in whom
his faculty of veneration may find satisfaction. The days
when there was no king in Israel, and every man did what was
right in his own eyes, were far from being either contented
or prosperous.

How remarkable it is that the Kingship of Jesus should
have been so accentuated in his trial! It was the centre
around which the storm raged. Pilate challenged his claims:
"Art Thou a king, then?" and Jesus asseverated them:
"Thou sayest that I am—a king." The faded purple robe
flung over his shoulders, the reed in his hand, the mocking
bending of the knee, the crown of thorns on his brow, were
but the grotesque and heartless mockery of his claims. And
when his sacred body was affixed to the cross, the title on the
headpiece, written in the languages of learning, imperial
power, and religion, attested that He was King of the
Jews.

And since He has passed into the glory, He is still the Priest-King. Not Aaron, but Melchizedek, is the true type of our Saviour now. As Aaron, He made atonement and propitiation for sin; but as Melchizedek, He has sat down at the right hand of the throne of God. "This Melchizedek was King of Salem, and Priest of the Most High God."

As Priest, Jesus pleads the merit of his blood; as King, He exerts power on our behalf. As Priest, He pacifies the guilty conscience; as King, He sends thrills of his own victorious life into our spirits. As Priest, He brings us nigh to God; as King, He treads out enemies under his feet. It is of great importance to us all to think of our Saviour in this dual aspect. On the one hand, we get all the benefit of his Cross and Passion; on the other, all the benefit of his resurrection and session at the right hand of God. May it not be that the weakness of thy Christian life is due to the fact that thou hast viewed Him only in the light of Calvary, and hast not, with Stephen, seen Him seated at the right hand of the Majesty on High—a Prince as well as a Saviour—a Saviour because a Prince? Thank God for the Lamb; but rejoice, O child of God, that He is in the midst of the throne! He bore the penalty of thy sin, when He shed his precious Blood; He will deliver thee from the power of sin, as thou placest thyself absolutely beneath his royalty, both King and Lord. When He is absolutely trusted and obeyed, He accounts Himself absolutely responsible to achieve the uttermost salvation of those who trust in Him. If there is some sin which defies *thee*, at least it shall not be too strong for *Him*. And if the outflow of his delivering power towards thee seems restrained and ineffective, be sure that, in some one particular, which He will be quick to show thee, if only thou art willing to be informed, there has been a failure to yield Him the obedience which is due to Him as thy King. He sits and rules upon the throne of the universe; and, therefore, will subdue all rule, authority, and power. He must sit and rule on the throne of thy heart, that there also He may put down everything which opposes and obstructs his sway. "God hath exalted Him to be a Prince and a Saviour." *Acts 5:31*

What majesty there is in these words: "He shall sit and rule upon his throne, and He shall be a Priest upon his throne"! Let all other beings stand; He sits. He sits *6:13* because of his intrinsic dignity; because of his finished mediatorial work; because full of a calm expectancy that his foes shall be subdued under Him. The priests of Aaron's line stood day by day ministering and offering oftentimes the same sacrifices, the which could never take away sins; but HE, "when He had offered one sacrifice for sins for ever, *Heb* sat down at the right hand of God, from henceforth expecting *10:13* till his enemies be made the footstool of his feet."

Infinite woe has come to mankind through the reign of priests. No rule has been so intolerant, so capricious, so cruel, as that exercised by some of the pontiffs, or by priests, of one sort and another, through monarchs, who have been the creatures of their will. But this world will never be at rest until it submits to the beneficent rule of the Lord Jesus, and acknowledges that the counsel of its peace emanates from the combination of these two offices in his sacred person.

III. As THE PRIEST-KING, CHRIST BUILDS THE TEMPLE OF GOD.—Twice over this is affirmed; but what untold comfort the assurance must have brought when first addressed to that little band of exiles! Their temple site was strewn with ruins : it seemed almost hopeless to contend with those heaps of rubbish, impossible to rear a fabric worthy of the past and adequate for the future ; but these words must have greatly heartened them. As the hand of Inspiration drew aside the vail, they beheld another and greater than either Joshua or Zerubbabel, working with them and for them, and bearing the chief responsibility in all the toils and labours of their

E

new erection—*He* ; not they. They would work with new energy and courage, knowing, as they did, that they were fellow-workers with God. What difficulty could daunt, what enemies thwart or frustrate, the work of his right hand ?

Is not this as true a description of what is happening to-day as it was of those far-off incidents of temple-building ? We may be engaged in building that spiritual house, that holy temple of saved souls, which is slowly rising amid the wrecks of time ; and sometimes it seems as though the structure will never be completed. The scaffolding poles and rafters hide the unfinished walls ; the very pattern is obscured amid the dust and pother ; for every step in advance there are apparently two or three of recession and failure, and we break our hearts. Will the work ever be done ? Is it worth all the expenditure of blood and tears ? Shall we not desist ?

Then we understand that we have much less to do with it than we supposed ; that we are not so necessary as we thought ; that we are but day labourers at the best, and that He is the great Master Builder. It was this that made Paul exclaim : "We are God's fellow-workers; ye are *God's* Husbandry, *God's* Building."

If these words should be read by any who are losing heart because of the difficulties presented by their parish, their church, or the souls of their charge, let them be reassured, as they behold the trowel in the hands of the Priest-King; and let them be sure that He will succeed. They know not what He is doing, or using them to do. They are probably doing more than they know; and He is responsible for employing them, whether in the deep foundation-digging, or in the high storeys away in the sunny air. But let them not be discouraged, or desert Him, lest He be compelled to summon others to help Him perfect what they commenced.

.   .   .   .   .

The crowns of gold were put aside till the Temple was completed, and then deposited there, as a memorial to the men who had formed the deputation ; and an assurance was given that those who were far off should come to add their strength to that of the returned remnant.

The spiritual Temple is rising through the ages, and includes the workmanship of Jew and Gentile, of bond and free, of those who are the children of privilege, and those who seemed outside the pale of salvation. "Remember that aforetime ye, the Gentiles in the flesh, . . . were, at that time, separate from Christ, alienated from the commonwealth of Israel, and strangers from the covenants of promise; . . . but now ye are fellow-citizens with the saints, being built upon the foundation of the apostles and prophets, Christ Jesus Himself being the chief Corner-stone, in whom the whole building, fitly framed together, groweth into a holy temple in the Lord."

IX

FASTS TURNED TO FEASTS
(ZECHARIAH vii., viii)

THE JEWS, during their captivity, appear to have observed
four fasts. Four months were darkened by them. That of the
tenth month recalled the first enclosure of Jerusalem by the
lines of circumvallation; that of the fourth month commemorated the capture of the city in the reign of Zedekiah
(Jer. xxxix. 2; lii. 6, 7); of the fifth, the disaster which capped
all, when the house of the Lord was set on fire (lii. 12–14);
that of the seventh, the murder of Gedaliah, resulting in the
dispersion of the remnant (xli. 1–3).

The Jewish year was thus filled with sad retrospects, and
the national life was perpetually oppressed with gloom: for
it is clear that the observance of these days was a rigorous
obligation (Zech. vii. 4–6).

On their return from captivity the people still maintained
these fasts; and it seems to have struck some of the exiles
who had settled in Bethel as altogether incongruous to
continue wearing sackcloth, and casting ashes on their heads,
when the Holy City was rapidly rising from the dust, and
regaining much of her former prosperity and beauty. It
seemed to savour of unreality and hypocrisy to continue to
profess a grief which had long since been assuaged, and even
changed into great joy. Surely the confessions and lamentations, which were befitting enough in Babylon, were out of
place in the land of their fathers. They sent, therefore, a
deputation to the house of God, to consult the priests and
prophets congregated there, saying: "Should I weep in the

fifth month, separating myself, as I have done these so many years ?" (Zech. vii. 1–3).

It was a very reasonable inquiry, and becoming to honourable men, who felt that fasting and mourning must be both meaningless in themselves and displeasing to God, unless they were the outward expression of the soul's genuine emotions. It was surely worse than useless to keep up an antiquated form, the effigy of the past, the withered mummy of a service which once expressed the most profound anguish and repentance. It is, above all things, necessary to be real in our religious life—never to profess what we do not feel. Do not keep up a form for form's sake, if you have left behind the experience of which it was once the expression. Nothing will so deaden the soul as the maintenance of rites from which the fire and light have died, leaving them as the *scoriæ* of the volcano.

Zechariah seems to have given four separate answers to this inquiry. Four times "The word of the Lord of Hosts" came to him.

In the first (vii. 4–7), he reminds the people that these fasts were of their own appointing; and suggests the inference, therefore, that as they had inaugurated them, they were at liberty to discontinue them when they chose. He suggests the further inference, also, that it would have been far better if, instead of appointing fasts, which satisfied national sentiment, the people had set themselves to ponder the words of the older prophets: "Should ye not hear the words which the Lord hath cried by the former prophets, when Jerusalem was inhabited, and in prosperity?" It is so much easier to set up fasts and to insist on outward observances, than to bow down the heart before God, and to obey the ordinances which He has enjoined.

In the second (vii. 8–14), the prophet says, that whatever they may or may not do with respect to the outward fast, they should at least exemplify the spirit of true religion, which was of priceless importance. "Execute true judgment, and show mercy and compassion every man to his brother; and oppress not the widow, nor the fatherless, the stranger, nor the poor; and let none of you imagine evil against his brother in your heart." Thus had God spoken to their fathers, and thus He was now speaking with them. Their fathers had refused to hear, but had made their hearts as an adamant stone; and it had befallen, therefore, that, as they were deaf to God's cry, so He had been to theirs. He had scattered them as with a whirlwind, and left their land desolate. Thus Zechariah implored the people of his time not to yield to the obtuseness and disobedience of their fathers; that they might escape their fate, and that no catastrophe should interrupt the resurrection of their nation, or cast it back into the disasters with which it had been visited.

In his third answer (viii. 1–17), Zechariah dilates on the great prosperity which was awaiting the chosen city. The Lord had returned to dwell there, to constitute Jerusalem the city of truth, and Zion, his holy mountain. The streets should yet be full of old men and women, staff in hand for very age. The ringing, careless laughter of boys and girls at play should proclaim the prosperity and security of the times. From east and west, contingents of exiles should troop back to repopulate the former desolations. "Now I will not be unto the remnant of this people as in the former days, saith the Lord of Hosts. For there shall be the seed of peace; the vine shall give her fruit, and the ground shall give her increase, and the heavens shall give their dew; and I will cause the remnant of this people to inherit all these things."

And, again, on these delightful promises ensue the reiterated appeals—that every man should speak truth with his neighbour; that true judgment should be executed in the gates; and that all things which God hated should be put away. It was as though these golden visions of prosperity

and blessedness were enumerated to convince the chosen
people that God desired to remember their sins no more;
and to urge that, instead of dwelling mournfully on the past,
they should launch upon the swelling tide of light and love,
which was creeping up their shores.

This is God's way still. He chastens sorely. If we profane
his name and pollute his Temple; if we strike hands in
ungodly alliances, and go after strange gods; if we dye our
hands in the vats of the world's vanity—we are sent, as Israel
was, into captivity, and our seventy years are fulfilled. But
when we have profited by his stern discipline, and returned
to Him with all our heart and soul, we are restored to our
former position; God's hand wipes the tears from our eyes,
and He bids us turn from our bitter repinings over an
irretrievable past, to accept the unalloyed mercy which
remembers our sins no more:

> God who, whatever frenzy of our fretting
> Vexes sad life to spoil and to destroy,
> Lendeth an hour for peace and for forgetting,
> Setteth in pain the jewel of his joy.

Such dealings with his rebellious and erring children are
very wonderful. They pass all human thought. It is much
to be forgiven: but to be forgiven so utterly, so completely,
so extravagantly, "according to the riches of his grace"—
here is a marvel indeed. But there is no marvel with Him!
Such grace is no effort to his glorious nature! He is not
sensible of strain! It is simply the bubbling over of his
heart, which is Love. "Thus saith the Lord of Hosts: If it
be marvellous in the eyes of the remnant of this people,
should it also be marvellous in mine eyes, saith the Lord
of Hosts?" "His ways are higher than our ways, and his
thoughts than our thoughts."

In his final answer (viii. 18–23), Zechariah gives a delightful anticipation of future days, which are still awaiting

complete realization, but in some measure were fulfilled in the history of the Restoration. "The word of the Lord of Hosts came unto me, saying, Thus saith the Lord of Hosts: The fast of the fourth month, of the fifth, of the seventh, and of the tenth, shall be to the house of Judah joy and gladness, and cheerful feasts; therefore love the truth and peace" (viii. 18, 19).

This is a welcome exchange. We could not be surprised to learn that God had so blotted out the memory of the past that fateful anniversaries would pass without special recognition. Our memory of the dark and disastrous is commonly short-lived. Bitter recollections soon fade from memory's tablets. What we do not like to recall, we drop into the keeping of oblivion, and that sea is never in haste to give up its dead. But the remarkable point here was, that these anniversaries, which had formerly brought the deepest melancholy, would henceforth be hailed as festal days; as though the events which had happened on them, and seemed only disastrous, were really full of the choicest blessing, and had been misinterpreted. It reminds us of the dark lines in the spectrum, which stand for new and unrealized constituents in the solar atmosphere. Does the astronomer regret them, when he understands their significance? No; he counts them of inexpressible worth.

As we inquire how such a revulsion of feeling could be brought about, we catch a further glimpse into God's thoughts. He set Himself to assure his people, in effect, that in the future, when they could view his dealings in their true perspective, they would discover that their darkest days had been the source and origin of their gladdest ones; because through them they had come to know themselves, been weaned from their sins, and had acquired those virtues which attracted the reverence and love of the world.

Consider again these glowing predictions: "It shall come to pass that as ye were a curse among the nations, O house of

Judah and house of Israel, so will I save you, and ye shall be a blessing." And again: "Thus saith the Lord of Hosts, It shall yet come to pass, that there shall come peoples, and the inhabitants of many cities; and the inhabitants of one city shall go to another, saying, Let us go speedily to entreat the favour of the Lord, and to seek the Lord of Hosts." And again: "Thus saith the Lord of Hosts, In those days it shall come to pass that ten men shall take hold, out of all the languages of the nations, shall even take hold of the skirt of him that is a Jew, saying, We will go with you, for we have heard that God is with you" (verses 13, 20, 23).

These predictions have already been marvellously fulfilled. In the midst of the dark night of heathen idolatry, when the foremost and wisest nations of the world were given up to the grossest idolatry and impurity, the synagogues of the dispersed Jews shone like sparks of light, holding forth the great doctrines of the unity and spirituality of the Divine Nature, the need of forgiveness, and the sanctity of Home. In every considerable Gentile city, the synagogue had a large following of devout proselytes drawn from the leading Gentile families. From the Jewish nation came the Saviour of mankind, and the earliest members of his Church. To Jews we owe the New Testament, as well as the Old. It was at Jerusalem, on the occasion of a Jewish festival, that the Holy Ghost descended to begin his mighty work. And in all the so-called Christian ages, whilst persecuting the chosen people, the foremost nations of the world have taken hold of their skirts, going with them to their sacred shrines, using their conceptions of God, appropriating their sacred writings, and venerating their lawgivers, prophets, and saints, with a reverence equal to their own.

There is also a time, yet future, but probably not far away, when the Jewish people shall be brought to own the claims of Jesus, and shall look on Him with repentance, faith, and love; and then they will be still more sought after by the nations of the world as the representatives and teachers of the only true religion. These days are clearly predicted; and the signs on every hand corroborate our faith that it shall be even as the prophets, and this prophet especially, have foretold.

But we can never forget that this vast respect of the world for the Jewish people 'dates from the Babylonish captivity. Before that they were too fickle in their allegiance to Jehovah, too deeply tarred by the vile impurities of surrounding peoples, to win either audience or credence, when they advocated their own religion. What respect could the nation have for them, when the heights around Zion were covered by temples to foreign deities; and when the same defiling rites were practised, as disgraced the fanes of Chemosh, Molech, and Astarte? Abana and Pharpar were equal to any of the waters of Israel; Balaam was as Moses, and Zoroaster as Elijah.

But the captivity altered everything. They entered it deeply imbued with polytheism, and left it the strictest monotheists the world has ever seen. Their sorrows gave birth to some of their noblest Scriptures, and made their hold on the sacred Canon more tenacious than ever. Cast out by man, they fled to the bosom of God. Divorced from the outward rites of the Temple, they were driven to cling to the spiritual realities, of which the Levitical institutions were only transient types. Israel owes all the influence she has wielded in the world to the anguish which culminated in the conflagration of the Temple; and, if she were wise, she would evermore keep those ancient anniversaries of despair as birthdays of her power. Until March, the farmer may regard with regret the days in which he empties his barns of their precious contents to cast seed into the soil; but when April comes, and all the furrows are covered with the green spires of the young corn, he reviews those dark winter days with congratulation, and dates from them his glorious heritage.

From this historical review, we are led to apprehend the working of an eternal principle, which is thus enunciated elsewhere by the Holy Spirit: "Now no chastening for the present seemeth to be joyous, but grievous; nevertheless, afterward it yieldeth the peaceable fruits of righteousness with them that are exercised thereby."

We have all had our dark, sad days. The day when God said "No" to some eagerly pressed request; or when life was overcast by a dread announcement concerning our own life, or the life of one dearer to us than life; or when our trust in man's faith rocked to ruin. We have put a black mark against those days in our calendar, and are apt, as these anniversaries occur, to give ourselves to unrestrained sorrow. It is natural, and God does not blame the tears which are salt with rebellious repining. It is natural and human, as we sit by the crags on which the sea breaks heavily, to regret the tender grave of a day that is dead, and to long for the sound of a voice that is still, and to borrow from Job's magnificent soliloquy:

Let that day be darkness;
Let not God regard it from above,
Neither let the light shine upon it.

Let darkness and the shadow of death claim it for their own. But this will not be our final verdict. Probably in the golden sunset of our life, when we can see its true meaning and perspective, when its various parts are fitted together like the variously-shaped pieces of our childhood's puzzles, we shall see reason to thank God most for our darkest days, so long as they are not days of sin, and to keep them as feasts in the eternal noon of heaven. We shall perceive that out of the darkness light was born; out of the anguish joy was born; out of the trial we entered into God's blessed peace.

That day, when God said "No" to your hot desires, was the day of your weaning from the babe-life into the strength and growth of an independent existence. That day, when a dark cloud settled on all your hopes, was the beginning of your new appreciation of the eternal constellations, shining unnoticed in your sky. That day, when your Joseph was torn from you, was really necessary to those seventeen years of prosperity in the sunshine of Eygpt's favour. That day of·captivity, which snatched you from your busy life, to share Paul's four years' imprisonment at Cæsarea and Rome, gave birth to deeper views of the nature of Jesus; so that, whereas you had only known Him as the Divine Substitute, you came to know Him in his heavenly glory, seated at the right hand of God; and your discoveries not only comforted your stricken heart, but made for the enrichment of the world.

Dare to believe this; dare to anticipate the far-off interest of tears; dare to live in the day which is after to-morrow. As Dante said, "In God's will is our peace." He loves us infinitely. No good thing will He withhold. He must lay deep in tears the foundations that shall upbear our eternal weight of glory:

> *Thus hath He done, and shall we not adore Him?*
> *This shall He do, and can we still despair?*
> *Come, let us quickly fling ourselves before Him—*
> *Cast at his feet the burden of our care.*

X

GOOD NEWS FOR PRISONERS OF HOPE
(ZECHARIAH ix)

THERE is a change in the phraseology of the remaining chapters of this book. Not now *the word of the Lord,* but *the burden of the word of the Lord.* By this term we are prepared for tidings of sorrow and disaster, which are about to fall on the nations addressed. These burdens lay heavily on the soul of the prophet, who was probably already advanced in years when he announced them. There is, at least, a remarkable contrast between the *visions* of the earlier and the *predictions* of the later chapters. The difference has even led some critics to suppose that they were added by another hand; but this view, founded rather on internal evidence, cannot be maintained in the face of the strong external testimony for the unity of the authorship of this book.

When Zechariah wrote this prophecy, the early troubles of the returned remnant in the reconstruction of Temple, City, and State, were at an end; but they were hemmed in and pressed by Tyre on the north, and by Ashkelon, Gaza, and Ekron on the south. It was for their encouragement, therefore, that he foretold an approaching invasion, before which their strong and hostile neighbours would be swept away. Though Tyre had built herself a stronghold on an apparently impregnable island, and heaped up silver as the dust, and fine gold as the mire of the streets; and though her counsellors were famous for their wisdom—the Lord would dispossess her, smiting her power in the sea, and devouring her palaces with fire. And the devastation which would befall Damascus and Hadrach (a part of Syria) would extend southwards till the worst fears of Gaza, Ashkelon, and Ekron would be realized in their utter destruction. Philistia would be as a young lion deprived of its prey, whilst the chosen city would be defended by unseen angel forces. "I will encamp about mine house as a garrison, that none pass through or return; and no oppressor shall pass through them any more; for now have I seen with mine eyes."

All these predictions were literally fulfilled within a few years by the invasion of the third of the great world-conquerors, Alexander the Great. Syria, New Tyre, and the old seaboard, including the cities of Philistia, fell under his arms; but both in going and returning, he spared Jerusalem, being much impressed by a dream, in which he was warned not to approach the city, and by a solemn procession of priests and Levites, headed by Jaddua, the high priest.

Then a stream of exalted prediction ensues, sweet as the refrain of an angel's hymn, which, as the Evangelist tells us, was fulfilled when, in lowly triumph, Jesus entered Jerusalem at the beginning of the week in which He died. "This came to pass, that it might be fulfilled which was spoken through the prophet, saying, Tell ye the daughter of Zion, Behold, thy king cometh unto thee, meek, and riding upon an ass, and upon a colt, the foal of an ass." What sublimity there is in the prophet's words, in which stress is laid on the fact that the King who saves is lowly; that his steed is not the richly-caparisoned war-horse, but the humble ass; and that He needs neither chariot nor battle-bow for the overthrow of his foes; but speaks peace unto the nations, as though waving his hands in priestly benediction over the troubled waters; and lo, there is a great calm (verses 9, 10).

Then follows the remarkable promise alluded to in the heading of this chapter. "As for thee also, because of the blood of thy covenant I have sent forth thy prisoners out of the pit wherein is no water. Turn you to the stronghold, ye prisoners of hope; even to-day do I declare that I will render double unto thee."

In eastern lands, liable to long spells of drought, it is customary to hew cisterns out of the solid rock for the storage of water, that provision may be made against the failure of the rains. These abound in Palestine. "They hewed out for themselves cisterns." When these were empty, they might be used for other purposes, and at all times provided a useful retreat, or hiding-place, from the Philistines or other hostile neighbours, who periodically poured up through the valleys, carrying fire and sword to the peaceful pastoral and agricultural hamlets. Such use of the rock-hewn cisterns is referred to in these words. It seemed to the prophet as though Israel might be compared to a terrified peasantry, sheltering in some dark, dry, mountain cistern, far up from the valleys, dreading every day lest their hiding-place might be discovered, and themselves dragged forth to dye with their blood the green sward.

Thus, in every age God's people have been imprisoned. You may have been caught in the snare of this world's evil. You have no sympathy with it, yet somehow you have become involved in the snares and toils of malign combinations. As the wild thing of the forest, bounding carelessly down the glade, suddenly finds itself at the bottom of the dark pit prepared and hidden by the hunter; so you, who began life so guilelessly, and passed your early days so blithely, have awoke to discover yourself involved with people and things, from which you cannot dissociate yourself. You have no desire for them—they chafe and try you—but you cannot get off. It seems as though some evil spirit has lassoed you, not indeed in your soul, but in your home and circumstances.

Or, perhaps, you have been led captive by the devil at his will. There is no doubt about your sonship; in your better moments, God's Spirit witnesses clearly with yours that you have been born again; you have strong yearnings after the souls of others, and at times are marvellously used for their awakening and comfort: and yet, during long and sad periods of experience, you seem the bound slave of the great enemy of souls; swept before strong gusts of passion; careening in the dock; water-logged until progress in the divine life seems impossible, and you can only drift helplessly to and fro on the tides.

Or, perhaps, you have fallen into deep despondency, partly as the result of ill-health, and partly because you have looked off the face of Christ to the winds and waves. The clear-shining of his love is obscured, and at times it is difficult to believe in anything but the pressure of your own dark thoughts. Some of God's children seem to choose the valley of the shadow of death as the site of their dwelling, and then employ doubt, dread, and despondency, to design and build the house, which is sadly like a gaol. They affect the sombre tint, and the despairful tone; and—strange anomaly!— appear happiest when abandoned to the profoundest melancholy.

All such are prisoners, but they are prisoners of hope. There is a sure and certain hope of their deliverance. Out of their prisons they shall ultimately emerge, as Peter, angel-led, from his. The clouds might more easily succeed in imprisoning the sun than any of these dark conditions permanently hold one of God's children. They belong to the light and day; and, though they see it not, Hope, as God's angel, is standing near, only waiting his signal to open the prison door. The prisoner, on whom the sentence of capital punishment has been passed, and who has no strong, wise friends to interfere on his behalf, may well abandon hope as he passes within the massive walls of the fortress, and hears the heavy gates, one after another, slammed and locked behind him. But where justice and truth are on his side, when he has been the victim of craft and guile, if there be a good wife and strong friends to espouse his cause, though he be incarcerated, bound with chains on the Devil's Island, and though the weary years pass over him, yet he is a prisoner of hope, and shall come forth again into the light of day. All God's children are prisoners of hope.

Their hope rests on the Blood of the Covenant. "Because of the blood of thy covenant, I have sent forth thy prisoners out of the pit." When God entered into covenant-relationship with Abraham, the sacred compact was ratified by the mingled blood of an heifer of three years old, a she-goat of three years old, a ram of three years old, a turtle dove, and a young pigeon. And, in after years, when, beneath the beetling cliffs of Sinai, Moses acted as mediator between God and the children of Israel, he sent young men, because the order of priesthood was not established, which offered burnt-offerings and sacrificed peace-offerings of oxen unto the Lord. Then Moses took the blood and sprinkled part on the altar, and part on the people, saying, "Behold the blood of the covenant which the Lord hath made with you concerning all these words" (Gen. xv. 9; Exod. xxiv. 7, 8).

Similarly, when the new covenant—the provisions of which are enumerated in Heb. viii—was ratified, it was in the blood of Jesus. As He took the cup, He said: "This is my blood of the new covenant, which is shed for many unto the remission of sins." "And for this cause He is the Mediator of a new covenant." The shedding of the blood of the Lamb of God indicates that God has entered into a covenant relationship with Him, and all whom He represents, who are, by faith, members of his mystical body, the Church. On his side, He promises to be a God to us, and to take us to be his people; on our side, Christ promises, on our behalf, that we shall be a people for his own possession, zealous of good works. This covenant embraces all who have believed, shall believe, and do believe in Jesus. It embraces thee, if thou dost at this moment simply believe in Him as thine, and art willing to be evermore his. And in placing the cup to thy

F

lips at the Holy Supper, thou dost visibly and solemnly attest thy belief that there is a special relationship between God and thee, not in virtue of thy worthiness, but for the sake of his Son, that great Shepherd, who, through the blood of the everlasting Covenant, was brought again from the dead.

Because of the Blood of the Covenant, God will send forth each of his imprisoned ones out of the pit. That blood binds Him to interpose on their behalf. Wherever they are, and however thick-ribbed the walls of their prison, God must deliver them. That they might have strong consolation, He has confirmed his word by an oath. He will bow the heavens and come down, will ride upon a cherub and fly, will certainly rescue from the entanglements and complications of evil.

Suppose two men were bound in the closest, tenderest friendship, not needing to exchange blood from each other's veins, as the manner of some is, because heart had already exchanged with heart; and suppose one of these, travelling in Calabria or Anatolia, was captured by brigands and carried into some mountain fastness, threatened with death unless ransomed by an immense sum of money: can you imagine his friend at home, in the enjoyment of opulence and liberty, settling down in circumstances of ease, and allowing his brother to suffer his miserable fate, with no effort for his deliverance? It is impossible to imagine such a thing! With tireless perseverance, he would leave no stone unturned, and the captive might rely on every possible effort being made for his deliverance. So it is with God. Whatever be the sad combination of disaster which has overtaken us, He is bound by the Holy Covenant, sealed by the blood of Jesus, to spare no effort till our soul is escaped as a bird from the snare of the fowler, until the snare is broken, and we are escaped.

There is a remarkable illustration of this in the story of the conquest of Canaan. By guile, the men of Ai betrayed

Israel into making a covenant with them. Three days after
their lie was exposed; but the princes said, "We have sworn
unto them by the Lord, the God of Israel; now, therefore,
we will not touch them." And when Ai was besieged by
neighbouring kings, out of pure revenge, and an appeal was
made for help, it was at once furnished, because of Israel's
troth. So, child of God, if you have made Jesus your King,
He is sure to succour you. Behold, thy King cometh, O
prisoner of hope! He is just, and therefore he has salvation.

Is not this the reason why some of us are not delivered?
We should be glad enough to accept deliverance, but are
not prepared to pay the price. We have not observed the
divine order, and crowned Jesus King of our hearts and
lives. We are wishful that he should be our Saviour, but
not altogether prepared to accept Him as King. This is
our mistake; God hath exalted Him to be a Prince and a
Saviour; He is first King of Righteousness, before He is Priest
after the order of Melchizedek: and it is only when we con-
fess with our mouths Jesus as Lord, that we shall be saved.

But do not fear Him. His footfall is very soft. He is
lowly, and rides upon a colt, the foal of an ass. No prancing
steed, no banner flaunting in the breeze, no long train of
warriors. Soft as the summer breeze; irresistible as the
summer sunshine, before which great tubular bridges bend.
Lowly as a child—thy King, thy King is here! And before
his advent the bars are broken, as though ice were thawing
drop by drop in spring, and letting the imprisoned ship
through the close-set floes.

The King speaks peace; but He uses his emancipated
ones as weapons in the great fight. "I have bent Judah for
me" (as a man might bend his bow); "I have filled my bow
with Ephraim" (as with an arrow). This, in the first instance,
refers to the struggle of the Maccabees against Alexander's
successor—Antiochus—as appears in the following words:
"I will stir up thy sons, O Zion, against thy sons, O Greece,

and will make thee as the sword of a mighty man." But there is a deeper meaning, which applies to us all—Jesus first saves us, and then we become as arrows in the hand of a mighty man.

O prisoners of hope, lift up your heads ! your salvation is come out of Zion. Turn you to the stronghold ! The enemy has been driven from his position. There is no more fear of his attack. Take up your abode in the stronghold of God's care and love, in the fortress of his Righteousness, in the keep of his Covenant.

As we turn from this chapter, we cannot but feel that it contains unexplored depths, which no previous fulfilment has exhausted ; and which are probably awaiting further developments, which, at present, we cannot prognosticate. When the closing verses tell us of what God will do for his people, "seen over them," "defending them," "saving them, as the stones of a crown glittering on high over his land"; when our attention is called to the greatness of his goodness and beauty reflected on the people of his choice—we cannot but feel that days are coming in which He shall yet more conspicuously and victoriously interpose on their behalf, and when, literally, his dominion shall be from sea to sea, and from the river to the ends of the earth. And if such a surmise be true, this chapter is closely related to the scenes which are delineated in the last chapters of this book, and which probably lie just in front of us, waiting for the withdrawal of the veiling curtain, which often appears to move with preparations for the events behind it.

XI

GOD'S SOWINGS
(ZECHARIAH X)

To THE superficial eye there is no difference in the distance from our earth of the planets and the fixed stars; but, as a matter of fact, between the one and the other there is a vast intervening space of millions of miles. So in regard to these predictions. The prophet searches "what manner of time" the Spirit of Christ which is in him signifies. He describes the great facts revealed to him; but it is not within his province to announce the times and seasons which the Father hath kept in his own power. He sees the mighty mountain ranges; but it is left for us to discover that deep and far-stretching valleys lie between the nearer and the further, between the first and second advents of Christ. We shall find, therefore, the prophet passing from the one to the other, and grouping on the foreground of his picture incidents which really belong to different ages in the world's history. Such a method of workmanship was necessary, if prophecy was to be an incentive to faith and patience.

We have already had an illustration of this in the previous chapter, when the advent of the Christ on his lowly steed, the struggle of the Maccabees, and the deliverance of Israel in the last years of this dispensation, are classed together as though pertaining to the same epoch. There is nothing surprising in such grouping, if we remember that our Lord inserts the whole Christian dispensation in the break of a single comma (compare Isa. lxi. 2, and Luke iv. 19).

In this chapter and the next, taken as one, we detect the same fact. We are bidden, in the first verse, to ask for the latter rain, that Pentecost which is to close the present age, and which the apostle Peter describes as "times of refreshing from the presence of the Lord." These are to be expected, he tells us, when the Jewish people repent and turn again to God, and will inaugurate the time of restitution of all things, whereof God hath spoken by the mouth of his holy prophets, which have been since the world began. And the rest of the chapter may be interpreted as referring to the same events. But the next deals with the destruction of the second temple by Titus, and the rejection of the true Shepherd. In the thirteenth chapter there is a similar rapid transition from the final cleansing of the chosen people to the awaking of the sword against the Shepherd, who is also the fellow of the Lord of Hosts. And probably there is no satisfactory clue to the comprehension of the Lord's closing utterances about the fall of Jerusalem, which does not recognise the same principle. He passes from the close of the one age to that of the other, describing both in the same sentences; and only in a passing phrase, as when He speaks of the fulfilment of the times of the Gentiles, does He open to our view the mighty gulf of time which was destined to intervene.

If these thoughts are borne in mind, there will be no obstacle to our deriving help and teaching from these chapters; and in the last days of this dispensation we shall be able, with tolerable accuracy, to assign the various paragraphs to their respective place on the great chart of God's providential government.

From the summons to ask for the latter rain, coupled as it is with the Divine promise of a gracious hearing, we are led to a graphic description of what God will make of his people—a description which was partially realized in the successful stand made by Judas Maccabæus and his brethren against Antiochus. "Judah was as his goodly horse in the battle. From him came forth the corner-stone, from him the nail, from him the battle-bow, from him every exactor

together." The following description of their successes
against their foes, treading them down in the battle as mire
in the streets, was fully verified during that brief but glorious
period, when for a little the waning splendour of the Hebrew
people shone out in its pristine beauty. But when the prophet
goes on to class Joseph with Judah; and to speak of the
people being brought again from the ends of the earth, the
mightiest nations being humbled for their sake; and the pro-
mised land, though inhabited to Lebanon on the north,
and to Gilead on the east, being too small for them; we feel
that there looms before his vision something greater than has
taken place, or shall take place, till God summons his people
from all the world to inhabit their own land—as the bee-
farmer hisses for his bees, scattered in search of honey
throughout meadows and garden (verse 8).

In the meanwhile, during the present age, we may view
the Jewish race as so much buried seed. "I will sow them
among the people: and they shall remember Me in far
countries; and they shall live with their children, and shall
return."

At the end of the seventy years' captivity the people of
God's ancient choice were distributed through Parthia, Media,
Persia, Mesopotamia, Cappadocia, Pontus, Phrygia, Pam-
phylia, Egypt, Libya and Rome, Crete and Arabia. Everywhere, throughout the great Roman Empire, they fell into
the ground to die. So far as their natural life was concerned,
they seemed on the point of being obliterated among the
nations of the world; but you might as well talk of the ob-
literation of the seed which the husbandman casts into the
autumn furrows. They built their synagogues, throve in the
quarters assigned to them in the great cities, and disseminated
new conceptions of God, high ethical standards, a fresh
religious speech, destined to be of incalculable service to the
early preachers of Christ's Evangel.

At this present hour *the Jews* lie sown among all the

nations of the earth. But they still live, or exist, with their children, and shall one day return. There shall be spring-time, earing, and harvest. The sea of affliction has too long rolled over them, with the thunder of its mighty billows. Its wide expanse has stretched out between them and their great destiny; but their Almighty Friend shall yet pass through it, smiting its waves and drying up its depths, achieving a national deliverance, so that they may reoccupy the land given in covenant to their fathers.

It was thus with the first believers. By the rough hand of the persecutor, the rich wheat of Pentecost, which had laid too long in the bin of the mother Church, was scattered abroad throughout the regions of Judea and Samaria. "They therefore that were scattered abroad went everywhere preach-ing the Word." "They therefore that were scattered abroad, upon the tribulation that arose about Stephen, travelled as far as Phœnicia, and Cyprus, and Antioch." These spring sowings yielded a marvellous return. There was such a crop of churches and converts as multiplied the original number of the Church a hundredfold. Though there was a diminu-tion of the numbers at Jerusalem, there were sheaves of golden corn throughout the world's acreage.

How many illustrations have existed, throughout *the entire history of the Church*, of the effect of God's sowings ! "My Father is the Husbandman," said our Lord. With both hands He has prosecuted his work of sowing. In the persecutions of Nero, Decius, and Diocletianus, the precious seed of the Kingdom was sown deep in the dark graves of agony and death. Surely the great Sower went forth weeping, as He bore the precious seed to its destined ministry. It was buried in the voracious animals of the arena, in the labyrinths of the catacombs, in the dens and caves of the earth; but it lived again in millions of converts that so filled the earth as to appal and silence their persecutors. The emperors at last gave up the work of slaughter, because martyrdoms only served to root Christianity deeper in the empire. The blood of the martyrs became the seed of the Church.

There was a grand quality in the corn of the Waldensian Valleys, in the Paulicians, the Hussites, the Lollards, which was sown by the Master in the dungeons of the Inquisition, in mockings and scourgings, in bonds and imprisonment, in the fires of martyrdom, and in the current of swiftly-flowing rivers. But what harvests it all yielded! There was, for instance, the harvest of the Reformation in Germany, of the Huguenots in France, and of the Puritans in England. It would be impossible to compute the vast hosts of the true disciples of Jesus through the dreary Middle Ages, because the apostate Church has concealed their number and misrepresented their influence. But many pages of the Lamb's Book of Life must be filled with their names. "A great multitude which no man can number, of every nation, and tribe, and people."

So in later days. The martyrs of Uganda have yielded to-day three hundred Christian churches. The devoted labours of saintly missionaries in India, Burmah, China, and Africa, who fell into the ground of obscurity, and loneliness, and disappointment, and died among strangers, many of them prematurely or violently—have resulted in the salvation of myriads. There was a handful of corn in the tops of mountains, in the ledges, where the earth was deep and rich enough to admit of a grave being dug, and the fruit thereof has shaken like Lebanon.

In all probability many of *the children of God* who read these lines know what sowing means. They, too, have fallen into the ground to die. That obscure village in which your friends say you are buried; that humble position in which your powers are cramped and limited by neglect and confinement; that bed of suffering and weakness; that incessant demand to undertake menial and lowly drudging; that summons to leave home and friends, and sphere of successful labour, to become the companion of savage and illiterate people—all this is the grave, with its darkness and silence, in which God sows his people; not that they should abide there for ever, but that they should bring forth much fruit. You shall live through other lives. Your prayers and alms shall be a memorial before God, and the day shall reveal the wonderful ways in which you have no longer abode alone.

Listen to the complaint of the buried seed: "Lord, in trouble have we visited Thee. We have poured out our prayer when thy chastening was upon us. We have been with child; we have been in pain; we have, as it were, brought forth wind; we have not wrought any deliverance in the earth, neither have the inhabitants of the world fallen." And here is the Divine response: "Thy dead shall live; my dead bodies shall arise. Awake and sing, ye that dwell in the dust; for thy dew is as the dew of herbs, and the earth shall cast forth the dead."

Sowing means *death*. "Except a corn of wheat fall into the ground and die . . ." We must be prepared to die, not only to sins, and weights, and self-indulgences, but to our own notions of pleasing God, to our emotional life, to our self-congratulation at the results of Christian service, to the energy and enthusiasm of our devotion. The little corn of wheat must feel very disconsolate when it finds itself attacked by chemical agents lurking in the soil, that begin to tear at its integuments and strike their rapiers at its heart. It is sad at having to surrender its beauty of form, its sprightly nimbleness, its secret soul. Dying is not easy work. And when the process is prolonged, when the disintegration of the self-energy takes place by slow degrees, it is bitter to bear.

Sowing means *darkness*. Through long months the seed lies in darkness and has no light. Madame Guyon tells of prolonged seasons in which she lost all the joy of God, that she might be led to God Himself. It is a strange experience: "God removes all *conscious* experience of his grace, all power to work for him, and the very beauty of the Divine virtues." The soul does not fall away from God, because He is beside it whilst it treads the dark valley; but it goes ever deeper into the grave of Jesus—no song on its lips, no rapture at its heart, no ray of sunlight from the former sources of hope and consolation.

Sowing means *loneliness*. The corn of wheat falls into the ground to die, that it may not abide alone; but this dying is necessarily a long experience. Each man is born alone, and alone he dies. God will perhaps touch your friends, and you will be separated from them by misunderstandings; your home life, so that your dearest will be called from your side; your church relationships, and you will have to go forth without the camp, bearing his reproach. But there is no one who has left brethren, or sister, or father, or mother, or children, for Christ's sake, that shall not receive a hundred-fold in this time, houses, and brethren, and sisters, and mothers, and children; and in the age to come eternal life.

But God does not forget the buried seed. Can a woman forget her sucking child? Can a farmer forget the seed which at so much pains he flung abroad on the brown furrows? Can God forget those who have not counted their lives dear unto themselves, but for his sake have been killed all the day long, and counted as sheep for the slaughter? They shall be his, in the day that He shall make even his peculiar treasure.

In that wonderful ladder or scale of ascending prayer, of which we are informed in Hosea, we hear the heaven calling to God, the earth calling to heaven, and the corn, wine, and oil calling to the earth, and Jezreel (the sown) calling to the corn, wine, and oil. And as the result of these appeals, ringing through earth and heaven, He who had sown his people in the earth, has mercy on them, and says, Thou art my people; and they say unto Him, Thou art our God. "Doubtless Thou art our Father, though Abraham knoweth

us not, and Israel doth not acknowledge us: Thou, O Lord,
art our Father, our Redeemer from everlasting."

When the destined hour has come the buried seed hears
the call of spring to arise and come forth from her cell. The
voice that bade Lazarus come forth is heard deep down in the
recesses of the earth. That which was in the grave hears the
voice of the Word of God, and comes forth. How beautifully
the words of the prophet's vision lend themselves to the
metamorphosis of the spring: "So I prophesied as He
commanded me, and the breath came into them, and they
lived, and stood upon their feet, an exceeding great army."

Yes, buried ones, God does not forget your work and
the love which ye have showed toward his name, in that
ye have ministered to his saints, and still minister, though
your ministries be hidden from the admiration of the great
world. Your resurrection is guaranteed. You may not be
able to discover the body of usefulness with which you will
be clothed. God will give you your body as it pleases Him,
and to each its own. But your death shall be swallowed up in
the victory of life, and God shall wipe all tears from your
eyes.

And that new life will be God's. "They shall remember Me,
. . . and they shall live." Jesus said that he who believed in
Him, though he were dead, yet should he live. Now, to
believe is to receive. Evidently, then, the life which comes
after death is by the reception into our spirit of Him who is
the Resurrection and the Life. We obtain by union with
Jesus, and direct from God, all that we had previously
sought in his service, his gifts, his people.

"The soul lives no longer, works no longer of itself. It
is God (by the Holy Spirit) who lives, works, operates within
it. This goes on increasingly, so that it becomes rich with his
riches. It is also enriched and revivified by degrees as it was
stripped by degrees (2 Cor. iii. 18). The soul lives with the
life of God. He being the principle of life, it cannot want for

anything. It has lost the created for the Creator; nothingness for all things. All is given to it in God, not to possess, but to be possessed" (2 Cor. vi. 10; Col. ii. 9).

You have, as it were, been buried in Egypt; but God is going before you, smiting the waves of the sea and drying up the depths of the mighty river, which had seemed an impassable barrier. He will strengthen you to follow Him: only dare to step out in faith, and you shall walk up and down in his name (x. 12).

Who shall estimate the results? One head of corn may have fifty seed-corns, and each of these fifty, and each of these again fifty. At this rate, we may soon arrive at tens of thousands. Behold the revenue of your tears, and prayers, and anguish. God will richly compensate. Lift up thine eyes and see. They gather themselves together, they come to thee; thy sons shall come from far, and thy daughters borne in arms. The little one shall become a thousand, and the small one a strong nation, because the Lord will hasten it in his time.

XII

THE SHEPHERD OF ISRAEL
(ZECHARIAH xi. 1-17; xiii. 5-9)

IF THESE two passages are read together, it will be observed that they give some remarkable foreshadowings of the ministry of the Messiah to his flock of the chosen people, as well as to those other sheep of which He spake, as not of that fold, but which He must bring, that they should become one flock, one Shepherd (John x. 16).

Five hundred years before Judas sold the true Shepherd for thirty pieces of silver—the price of a slave—and then, seized with remorse, flung the price of blood upon the Temple pavement, that scene had been enacted in the streets of Jerusalem, freshly risen from their ruins. There is prophecy in action, as well as prediction; and the Holy Spirit often led the prophets to embody in striking deeds the conceptions of the future which had been impressed on their own minds.

At the time of which we write the Jewish people seem to have been specially unfortunate. Joshua and Zerubbabel had both passed away, and the rulers and priests who had succeeded them were actuated by the most violent passions. They resembled fire devouring the cedars of Lebanon, or the axe by which the oaks of Bashan are felled. They slew the flock for the fleece, and the people became a prey to their rapacious appetite for self-aggrandisement. "They that sell them say, Blessed be the Lord, for I am rich, and their own shepherds pity them not." Hand was raised against hand, the rich plundered the poor, the rulers (*his king*, verse 6) smote the land with their violence and injustice, and every weaker one was delivered over to the oppression of high-handed wrong.

It was under such circumstances that Zechariah felt called upon to become the shepherd of Jehovah's harried flock, and to stand in the breach which should have been filled by faithful and righteous men. Whether Israel generally recognised his pastoral authority does not appear; but he realized strongly the call of God, and fed the flock of slaughter, verily the most miserable of sheep (verse 7, R.V., *marg.*).

Two staves were in his hand: the one a club to beat back the beasts of prey; the other the crook, with which to extricate any of his charge that might be entangled in pit or thicket. The one was called Beauty, or Grace; the other Bands, or Union. These were the rod and staff of which David had sung in earlier days, and they represent God's perpetual attitude towards his sheep. He ever deals with them in abundant grace; He is united to them, as they should be united to each other, by the bonds of everlasting love.

Three shepherds, which probably stand for the threefold office of Priest, Prophet, and King, had already failed in the difficult work of restoring order to the disturbed and distressed land. There had been an inalienable disagreement between the Divine Spirit and them. "My soul was weary of them, and their soul also loathed Me."

After a brief effort to reclaim Israel for its true Shepherd, Zechariah renounced the attempt, saying, "I will not feed you: that that dieth, let it die; and that that is to be cut off, let it be cut off; and let them which are left, eat every one the flesh of another." He broke his staff of beauteous grace, and cut it asunder; as though the tender love of God had withdrawn from its long wrestle with indomitable pride and self-will. As he did so, the poor of the flock that gave heed unto him, knew that he was acting in accord with the word of the Lord (verse 11).

Then came the crucial test. The prophet challenged the people to appraise his services, to give him their estimate in money value. "I said unto them, If ye think good, give me my hire; and if not, forbear." This incident may have taken place in the Temple, as he stood with his remaining staff in hand, face to face with those that held priestly office, though they lacked the priestly heart. In contempt and scorn, they weighed out to him thirty pieces of silver, the price of a slave. "There, prophet of God," they seemed to say, "take that! Thy services are as worthless to the community as those of some obscure menial employed in the lowest service!" A goodly price indeed for a man's prayers and tears, for a heart of compassion, and a life of absolute self-surrender! "Cast it unto the potter," said the inner voice; and, as for this people, they shall pass into the hand of rulers, who shall eat the flesh of the fat, and drive them along paths so rough and flinty that their hoofs will be torn in pieces—a prediction which had a terrible fulfilment in the days of Antiochus and of Herod the Great.

Thereupon the prophet also broke in pieces the other staff, Bands, that the brotherhood between Judah and Israel might be broken in symbol, as afterwards in reality. How evidently that brotherhood is broken to-day! The Jews among us are the descendants of Judah and Benjamin; but where are the ten tribes?

In the following paragraph (verses 15–17) there is a further evident reference to the terrible reign of Antiochus, whose cruelties towards the Jews instigated the heroic uprising of the Maccabees and their adherents, and led to deeds of faith and prowess, which will be for ever famous in the annals of the world.

Five centuries passed, and Jehovah made one last effort to reclaim his wandering sheep, who were "distressed and scattered, as sheep not having a shepherd" (Matt. ix. 36). Full of grace and truth, fresh from the bosom of the Father, Jesus was sent to gather the flock, which had been scattered in the cloudy and dark day. It was already a flock of slaughter when He began his ministry. The dark shadows of that awful storm of disaster and destruction, which was, within a period of forty years, to sweep Mount Zion bare, had already commenced to brood ominously over the devoted race. If his gracious offices had been recognised and accepted, that slaughter might have been averted. With his staff of grace and his crook of love, the Good Shepherd might have brought his flock from out the dangers that threatened it, and realized the ancient prediction of Ezekiel: "I will feed them with good pasture, and upon the mountains of the height of Israel shall their fold be; there shall they lie down in a good fold, and on fat pasture shall they feed upon the mountains of Israel." But they would have none of Him. He would have gathered them as the hen her brood, yet they would not. Therefore He was compelled to break his rod and staff, and abandon them to the results of their sin. He was compelled to abandon his earnest endeavours, and, quitting the Temple, uttered the ominous words. "Behold, your house is left unto you desolate. For I say unto you, Ye shall not see Me henceforth till ye shall say, Blessed is He that cometh in the name of the Lord"—a prediction which probably refers to the period described in the last chapter of this book. As Jesus withdrew from the Temple, the last effort of Jehovah to save Israel as a nation was frustrated; the greatest of her prophets had failed, and the last barrier to the catastrophe of descending judgment was removed.

It was at this juncture that the nation was challenged to appraise the worth of the Saviour's ministry. Between Judas and the priests a monstrous bargain was struck. "They weighed unto him thirty pieces of silver." This meagre dole of the priests stands in grim contrast to the priceless gift of Mary's ointment, at which Judas cavilled; but for this, and so little as this, the Messiah was sold, betrayed, and done to death.

Rejected by his own—the people whom He ardently longed to save—and forsaken by his chosen followers, the Good

Shepherd went forth alone to meet the sword. Not the sword
of Caiaphas, or the priests; not the sword of Pilate, or the
Romans; not the sword of impending justice—but the sword
of righteous retribution for the sins of Israel, and the sins
of the world. Jew though He were by birth, He was more.
The Son of Man, the second Adam, the Lord from Heaven—
such are the designations placed on his head, like many
crowns. It was as the representative of the race that He went
to receive into his own heart the penalty which, like the sword
of Damocles, hanging by a hair, impended not over Jerusalem
alone, but over the world. He had heard the mysterious
summons sounding through the courts of the Temple, and
along the corridors of time, "Awake, O sword, against my
Shepherd, and against the Man that is my Fellow, saith the
Lord of Hosts. Smite the Shepherd."

That sword had flashed in the hand of the Cherubim at
the gate of Eden; had turned every way to guard the path
to the Tree of Life; had threatened to pursue the trans-
gressing pair, with its relentless edge. It was the sword of
justice, the two-edged sword of the Word of God, which
avenges disobedience with death. For four thousand years
it had slept in its scabbard, pacified, if we may say so, by
the Divine assurance that the mercy shown to men would be
reconciled with the due acknowledgment of the righteous
demands of a broken law. But it could not sleep for ever.
God's promise must be redeemed, and his guarantee made
good; and so, in the fulness of the time, Jesus was set forth
as a propitiation, showing the Divine righteousness in passing
over sins done aforetime, in the forbearance of God, and
enabling God Himself to be just, and the Justifier of those
that have faith in Jesus.

When our Lord was arrested in the garden, condemned
by his judges, and, finally, nailed to the cross; when his
heart broke with uncontrollable and unfathomed grief; when
the soldier took a spear and pierced his side—simultaneously

with these outward scenes there was the awakening of the
sword of Divine justice, which pierced and laid bare his heart.
"He was wounded for our transgressions. He was bruised
for our iniquities: the chastisement of our peace was upon
Him; and with his stripes we are healed." We cannot pene-
trate the deep mystery which veils the cross, or understand
how the suffering of the Shepherd could be counted as
equivalent to our bearing the results of our sins. It is difficult
to comprehend the transference of penalty from a sinful race
to the sinless Substitute. But it is impossible to read the
inspired statements that describe the death of Christ without
realizing that, in some way, which we shall, perhaps, understand in heaven, He met and satisfied the claims of violated
law, so that it can ask no more. The quotation of this verse
by our Lord Himself on the threshold of Gethsemane (Matt.
xxvi. 31) indicates, with unerring precision, its reference and
fulfilment; and we believe that because the sword was
plunged in his heart, it will sleep for ever. The law is magni-
fied and honoured, as it could not be by the destruction of a
race. However much we prize the death of Christ, our Lord,
as an example of patience and self-sacrifice, we must never
forget that He did for us what we never could have done for
ourselves in magnifying, satisfying, and honouring the claims
of the Divine law.

It is interesting to notice how our Lord quotes this
summons to the sword. The prophet hears it addressed
directly by the lips of God, "Awake, O sword, against MY
Fellow;" but in the thought of Jesus, it was not a dumb
and impersonal agent merely, with power of automatic or
self-prompted action, but an instrument in his Father's
hand. In his lips the quotation stands: "*I* will smite the
Shepherd." With Him there was no vague abstraction or
impersonality. It was not an attitude or quality of the Divine
nature, such as justice or righteousness, that drew the sword
from its scabbard, and plunged it in his heart. He even

refused to see Judas, Caiaphas, or Pilate. Passing by all these secondary causes, He sped into the very presence of the Father, and realized that the cup was mixed, the death of the cross arranged, and the sword wielded by Him. This enabled Him to bear his unutterable woe with yielded will and acquiescing heart.

In this, O child of God, learn a life lesson. In all anxieties, in troubles that men may cause to thee, refuse to consider thyself a prey of their wild will, as though thou wert a storm-driven leaf; but dare to believe that what God permits to come is his appointment, and that amid all the plottings and machinations of human malice runs a Divine purpose.

The infinite meaning and value of the death of the Cross are indicated by the three significant appellations with which the Sufferer is addressed.

MY SHEPHERD.—Mark that emphatic MY. It is as though Jehovah would contrast the Shepherd of his choosing with those that had been selected by human caprice. His Davids against the people's Sauls. From out of the family of man, God has drawn, and is drawing, certain who are attracted by a special affinity to his Son, wrought in them by his Holy Spirit; and these are accounted his flock, and are entrusted to his pastoral care. They were the Father's; but the Father has made them over to the Son, according to Christ's own words: "Thine they were, and Thou gavest them Me, . . . and these have known that Thou didst send Me." Distinguished from the rest of men—because they hear the Shepherd's voice, know, and follow Him—these enjoy immediately and intimately his pastoral care. He guides them over the wolds of time, feeding them on the green pastures, and beside the still waters; conducting them through darksome gorges and dangerous glens; defending them from lion and bear with rod and staff; and even in the realms of glory not ceasing to be their Shepherd. They follow Him even deeper into the heart of eternity, where the fountains of life first break forth into sight.

This thought for the sheep committed to his custody possessed the mind of the Great Shepherd on the night in which He was betrayed, when He went forth to meet Judas and the arresting band. Placing Himself between them and the frightened little group that cowered behind Him, He said, "If ye seek Me, let these go their way." If He had been an hireling, when He saw the wolf coming, He would have fled; but because He was God's Shepherd, He stood between his own and peril, as He always will do in every dark hour that may menace us between this and the safety of the gates of pearl.

We have a strong claim on Jesus, because He is God's Shepherd, the representative of the Divine care, the custodian of the Divine honour. In every prayer for help, we may remind Him that He stands to us as the gift and sponsor of the Divine faithfulness. He must be to us all that God Himself would be.

MY FELLOW.—When our Lord quoted this text in the upper room, as He rose to leave it, He stopped before He reached these words. But the omission was not due to any hesitation on his part to appropriate them. He knew that He was Jehovah's Fellow, else He would never have included the Father with Himself in the significant pronoun, *We*. "*We* will come and make our abode with Him." He counted not equality with God a prize to be grasped at. And it was the fact of his being Jehovah's Fellow that made his death of such infinite worth. Man could not have redeemed his fellow; but the Infinite Lawgiver Himself, taking to his heart the penalty of his own broken law, afforded it the greatest possible homage and satisfaction.

Surely there is a designed contrast between *Fellow* and *Hosts*. God is the Lord of many *Hosts*, in heaven, and earth, and sea; but He has only one *Fellow*. All the Hosts of angels and nature had not availed of the work for propitiation— this He must do Himself; and He did it in the person of Jesus.

THE MAN.—"*The Man* that is my Fellow." By his tears
and anguish, by the pains of death and the article of disso-
lution, his humanity was attested. And how real, how tender,
how near they make Him to us all. No man so abject and
sinful but may approach Him, when he is numbered with the
transgressors, and hangs in death between two malefactors.
Would you touch God through his Fellow, then touch yonder
dying Man. The gulf is bridged; the yawning chasm is
spanned. By the grace of the one Man we may now receive
the abundance of grace, and reign in life, here and hereafter.

Beware how you treat this blessed Man. Still men sell
Him for thirty pieces of silver; tread beneath their wanton
feet his precious blood; and do despite to his grace. Still they
prefer their thirty paltry silverlings to his matchless worth.
Would that their blind eyes were opened to see the matchless
glory and beauty of Him who stands at their door to knock.

The disciples were scattered when their Shepherd was
taken. He had foreseen this: "Behold the hour cometh,
yea, is come, that ye shall be scattered, every one to his
own, and shall leave Me alone." And it seemed as though
the hand of God was against them, to their utter undoing
in the dread hours that followed. But who shall tell the
woes that befell the chosen people that had rejected the
Messiah ! The disciples wept for but a little space and their
sorrow was soon turned into joy. But the Jews succumbed
beneath the woes, which, within forty years, befell their
nation. It came to pass in all the land, that two parts were
cut off, whilst the remainder passed through the fire, and have
been passing through it ever since. Nor can it be otherwise,
until they acknowledge Jesus as their true Shepherd, and
allow Him to fold them, and humble themselves to become
the people of his pasture, and the sheep of his hand.

XIII

THE SPIRIT OF GRACE AND SUPPLICATION
(ZECHARIAH xii, xiii)

THERE is unusual solemnity in these opening words, as though to assure us that there can be no doubts as to the sufficiency of the Speaker to carry into effect all that He is about to unfold. "Thus saith the Lord, which stretcheth forth the heavens, and layeth the foundation of the earth, and formeth the spirit of man within him."

The vision itself refers to a time yet future, though perhaps not far away, when the Jewish people shall have returned to their own land, but still in unbelief. Indeed, it is supposed by some that they will be in actual league with some awful impersonation of Antichrist, in accordance with Daniel ix. 27. For some reason, for the present veiled in mystery, the anti-Semitic hate with which some of the nations of Europe are already smitten will then become universal, "and all the nations of the earth shall be gathered together against Jerusalem." But their confederacy will be overwhelmed with infinite disaster. Such is the burden of this threefold affirmation:—

"Behold, I will make Jerusalem a cup of reeling unto all the peoples round about" (verse 2).

"I will make Jerusalem a burdensome stone for all the peoples" (verse 3).

"In that day will I make the chieftains of Judah like a torch of fire in a sheaf" (verse 6).

Immediately upon this, an assurance is given that in that awful day, more fully described in the succeeding chapter, the Lord shall save, and the Lord shall defend (verses 7, 8). In

clouds the long-rejected Messiah, accompanied by his Bride
—the Church—will appear to the succour of his brethren,
as Joseph interposed on the behalf of his; and, as they behold
Him seated at the right hand of power, and coming as He
told Caiaphas He would, in the clouds of heaven, they will
appropriate the old refrain, prepared by Isaiah for this very
occasion; when He shall swallow up death in victory, and
take away the reproach of his people from off all the earth :—
"Lo, this is our God; we have waited for Him, and He will
save us: this is the Lord; we have waited for Him, we will
be glad and rejoice in his salvation" (Isa. xxv. 9). "Behold,
He cometh with the clouds; and every eye shall see Him, and
they which pierced Him; and all the tribes of the earth shall
mourn over Him. Even so, Amen." Then the Lord Jesus
will slay the lawless one with the break of his mouth, and
bring Him to nought by the brightness of his coming. And
then the solemn and awful threatenings of this passage will
take effect: "It shall come to pass in that day, that I will seek
to destroy all the nations that come against Jerusalem."

Let us now turn from this side of the picture to consider the
threefold effect that this interposition will have on the Jews
themselves :—

"In that day shall there be a great mourning" (verse 11).

"In that day there shall be a fountain opened" (xiii. 1).

"It shall come to pass on that day, that I will cut off the
names of the idols out of the land" (verse 2).

I. A GREAT MOURNING.—Notice *the certainty* of this
announcement. "There SHALL be a great mourning in
Jerusalem." There is no hesitation in the prophet's speech.
He is as sure as the apostle Paul, when he says, "So all
Israel shall be saved." This is a solemn reflection for the
traveller, as he perambulates the streets of Jerusalem, or
visits the piece of ancient wall by which the Jews wail
weekly. There shall be a great mourning, not because the

Turk has desecrated the sacred places, nor because the ruins of bygone days affront with their yawning gaps, nor yet because of the bitter sufferings of the much-hated race; but each for personal rejection of the Messiah, who was driven through those streets and crucified without the gate.

The Comparison. "As the mourning of Hadadrimmon in the Valley of Megiddon." At this spot the good King Josiah, whose reign had been the only gleam of brightness in the period between the reign of Hezekiah and the downfall of the State, was done to death by the Egyptian arrows. Jeremiah, the prince of lamenters, lamented for Josiah, and all the singing men and singing women spoke of him in their lamentations. There never had been such universal and heartrending sorrow since Israel became a nation, as that which arose when the royal chariot drove through Jerusalem bearing his dead body for burial; but such grief is the only symbol adequate to express that coming national agony, when Israel shall look on her rejected Lord and mourn.

Yet another metaphor is pressed into service. The anguish with which a parent mourns for his only son, the bitterness of sorrow for a firstborn, is heartrending in any land, and among all peoples; but it is peculiarly so in an Eastern—a Hebrew home. Yet the bitter mourning which is one day to fill Jerusalem will be like that—as it was in the land of Egypt, when every family mourned over the death of its firstborn.

It will be *universal.* From the highest to the lowest of the court—for Nathan here stands for the youngest of David's sons; from the highest to the lowest of the priestly order— for Shimei stands for the least conspicuous of the priestly clans; all the people that remain shall be bowed in one common act of contrition. It is much to see one prodigal stricken with remorse—what will it be when a whole nation beats on its breast, and bewails its sins ! Every wind laden with dirges, all the open spaces black with prostrate forms,

all eyes wet with tears, the sombre shadow of the funeral
pyre flung over all.

It will be *lonely*! "Every family apart, and their wives
apart." *Excessive* grief seeks seclusion. It brooks no dis-
traction; it's attention is too absorbed with the object of its
agony to have thought for anything beside. It did not seem
surprising to her friends, when Martha arose from a house-
ful of mourners, and hastened away. They whispered, "It's
natural enough: she wants to be alone. She goeth to the
grave to weep there." So this mourning will isolate people.
Each will feel personally concerned; each will feel as though
chiefly reponsible; each will take to his own heart the cruci-
fixion of the Messiah, and will turn the *Miserere* into a wail
of personal confession. "*I* have sinned; *I* pierced his hands
and feet; *I* am of all men most miserable, and of all sinners
the chief."

*It will be due to a vision of the mediatorial sufferings of
Jesus.* "They shall look on Him whom they pierced, and
they shall mourn." There is no doubt as to the application
of these words, for as the beloved apostle stood beside the
cross, on which only the precious casket of the Jewel—the
body of our Lord—remained and saw the soldier pierce his
side, as the blood and water issued forth, he was reminded
by the Holy Ghost that this Scripture was being fulfilled
(John xix. 34–36).

This is the fact which the Spirit of God delights to use
for the breaking of our hard hearts. They are broken on
the broken heart of Jesus. They are pierced by the sight of
His piercing. They mourn when they look on Him whom
they pierced.

There are two kinds of sorrow—the one to death, the
other to life. The first considers the penalty of our wrong-
doing; the second the Person against whom the wrong has
been done. The one is largely selfish, dreading only the
scorpion whip and the sting of flame—it would cease in a

moment if these were withdrawn; the other is altogether regardless of consequences that may accrue to itself, and bitterly laments that shame and sorrow have been brought to the heart of Jesus, so true, so tender, so altogether lovely.

Sinners seeking forgiveness often appear to think that they must bring some meed of sorrow as a condition of acceptance with the Saviour. If only they can feel an adequate sorrow for sin, they may surely bring their tears as a price for his mercy, as a reason for his salvation. But we can never feel an adequate sorrow for sin. To wait for this will be to wait for ever. To postpone coming until the tear-bottles are full, will be to postpone for ever. Besides, the spiritual philosophy of the matter is that we shall never get the right sorrow for sin till we see Jesus, and are admitted into the intimacy of his love. The tears that we do not need to weep over come, not before, but after conversion. It was after the poor sinful outcast had been forgiven that she washed the Saviour's feet with tears. It was when Jesus turned and looked upon Peter that he went forth to weep bitterly. We must come to Christ as we are, not trying to realize what sin is, not seeking to be smitten with adequate grief, but just accepting his finished work and trusting Himself: after this will come the forth-pouring of our grief. The eyes that first look to Him for salvation may be tearless, but they will not long remain so. The first act may be largely one of the will; but the last will be of the emotions. When we have looked on Him whom our sins pierced, we shall mourn as one mourneth for his only son, and be in bitterness as one in bitterness for his firstborn.

Let us distinguish, then, between Repentance and Penitence. The one is the child of the will; the other of the heart. We repent when we turn from sin to Christ; we are penitent when we meet his eyes, as Peter did, and go out to weep bitterly. To repent is the definite act of the moment; but penitence will accompany us to the very gates of heaven, only to flee away before the light of eternal blessedness.

The Agent in producing this mourning is the Holy Spirit. "I will pour . . . the Spirit of grace and supplication." Conviction of sin is the special work of the Holy Spirit. He uses the truth as his sword, piercing to the dividing asunder of soul and spirit, of the joints and marrow. He particularly takes the truth of the sufferings and death of the Lord Jesus, and presents that to the conscience, pressing home the evil of rejecting such a Saviour, such pity, such holy, yearning love, until the soul understands what sin has cost the Lord, and melts, as icebergs do when they float down into Southern seas.

II. A FOUNTAIN OPENED.—On the day of Pentecost Peter pointed to those cleansing streams. "And Peter said unto them; Repent ye, and be baptized *every one of you* in the name of Jesus Christ, unto the remission of your sins; and ye shall receive the gift of the Holy Ghost." With marvellous force and eloquence John Bunyan brought out the force of those words, "*every one of you*." "But I struck Him on his head with the rod: is there any hope for me?" *Every one of you*, saith the apostle. "But I spat in his face: is there forgiveness for me?" Yes, is the reply, for *every one of you*. "But I drove the spikes into his hands and feet, which transfixed Him to the cross: is there cleansing for me?" Yes, cries Peter, for *every one of you*. "But I pierced his side, though He had never done me wrong; it was a ruthless, cruel act, and I am sorry for it now: may that sin be washed away?" *Every one of you*, is the constant answer. Repent, and turn again, that your sins be blotted out. The blood of Jesus Christ, God's Son, cleanseth from all sin. If the blood of bulls and goats, and the ashes of an heifer sprinkling the unclean, sanctify unto the cleanness of the flesh, how much more shall the blood of Christ, who, through the Eternal

Spirit, offered Himself without blemish to God, cleanse your consciences !

And as it was at the beginning of this era, so it shall be at its close—with this difference, that whereas then some few thousand souls only stepped into the fountain, at last a whole nation, the house of David and the inhabitants of Jerusalem, shall wash there and be cleansed. Then the words of the apostle Peter, spoken centuries ago in Solomon's porch, will be fulfilled, when Israel repents and turns again; her sins will be blotted out, and there will come times of refreshing from the presence of the Lord, and the restoration of all things, "whereof God spake by the mouth of his holy prophets which have been since the world began" (Acts iii. 21).

III. THE DESTRUCTION OF IDOLATRY.—The names of the idols will be cut off out of the land, and the prophets and unclean spirits will be caused to pass out of it. It is not enough for God to forgive. He must deal with the sources of all the waywardness and backsliding of his people. There will be, therefore, a strong and radical dealing with idols, prophets, and demons.

The thoroughness of these drastic measures is brought out in an imaginary vignette of a household scene in those happy days. It is supposed that the son of Godly parents, who have lately mourned for their sins apart, and been delivered from them, suddenly feels himself called upon to assume the *rôle* of a prophet. He encourages people to come to him to detect the culprit in some theft or murder, or to cause the rain to fall on the parched ground, or to perform magical rites over the sick, or call up the dead—to do, in fact, what Balaam wanted Balak to do, when he sent for him across the desert. The tidings come to his parents, who are so devoted in their adherence to God, that they would rather lose their child than allow him to pursue his evil, Goddishonouring work in their home. "It shall come to pass that, when any shall yet prophesy, then his father and his mother that begat him shall say unto him, Thou shalt not live; for thou speakest lies in the name of the Lord: and his father and his mother that begat him shall thrust him through when he prophesieth." It would not be possible to discover a stronger way of affirming the absolute transformation that will finally come over the Jewish people, when their devotion to God shall overpower their natural love to their children.

The passion against idolatry and false prophets would become so intense, that the practisers of arts which had imposed on the credulity of the people would be ashamed and afraid to own their profession. "The prophets shall be ashamed, every one of his vision, when he prophesieth, neither shall they wear a hairy garment"—this being the special dress of the sons of the prophets, by which they were at once recognised.

If a township of people should rise against a man suspected of being a prophet, he would vehemently protest that they were mistaken, and that he was no prophet. Trembling for his life, because so certain of the temper of his accusers, he would make any subterfuge to escape suspicion. "I am a tiller of the ground, for I have been made a bondman from my youth."

If, finally, in the pursuance of their hot inquiry, they discovered marks on his body, which indicated that he had been previously convicted and branded for following the calling of a prophet, he would rather assign them to the hands of his friends than dare to admit that he had ever been suspected of claiming to be a prophet. "One shall say unto him, What are these wounds between thine arms? Then he shall answer, Those with which I was wounded in the house of my friends."

This inquiry and reply have often been associated with the marks of the nails in the hands of Christ. But this is not the natural reading of the passage, which can only be attributed in the sense above given; the evident drift of the passage being to show that there will be such a revelation of the evil wrought by the prophets, and so strong an antagonism against them, that those suspected of being such will be prepared to evade the charge at any cost, knowing that if it is established against them they may expect but short shrift. This will be a deliverance indeed, which shall be radical and final. But if God is prepared to do so great and perfect a work for his ancient people, let us give Him no rest until He has utterly abolished our idols also, and purified us unto Himself—people for his possession, zealous of good works.

XIV

"THINGS WHICH MUST SHORTLY COME TO PASS"
(ZECHARIAH xiv)

IT IS impossible to regard this mysterious and sublime prophecy as having been already fulfilled. There is nothing in the story of the Maccabees, nor in the fall of Jerusalem beneath the arms of Titus, which at all adequately fulfils the conditions of the prophet's words. When have all nations been gathered together against Jerusalem in battle? When has the Mount of Olives rent in twain for the flight of the besieged? What day that has ever broken from the East has fulfilled the description of verses 6 and 7? At what time of their chequered history have the Jews gathered the spoils of their enemies in battle; gold and silver, and apparel, in great abundance? Of course, it is possible to put metaphorical and spiritualizing interpretations on all these touches. But to do so is to jeopardize the whole force and value of prophetic Scripture. If the predictions of the Advent of our Lord in the days of his humiliation were so literally fulfilled, why should we suppose that the predictions of his Second Advent in great glory must be treated as metaphor and trope? Surely we are justified by the minute accuracy of the former fulfilment to expect as exact a fulfilment of prophecies which are still awaiting accomplishment. When it is built, the new Jerusalem shall comply with every line of the Architect's plan, as communicated to the prophet.

Following, then, the successive features of the prophet's delineation, we learn that a time is coming when the nations of the world—which, to adopt a modern phrase, may indicate the concert of European powers—will be gathered against

Jerusalem in battle, that city being held by the Jews, as yet in unbelief. And we can hardly doubt that Zechariah is here anticipating the same events as are described by Ezekiel, when the great nations of the north come against "the land that is brought back from the sword, and gathered out of many peoples, upon the mountains of Israel, to take the spoil and to take the prey" (Ezek. xxxviii., xxxix).

At first this invasion shall be completely successful. "The city shall be taken, and the houses rifled, and the women ravished": hell let loose, and no restraint exerted on the excesses of the infuriated soldiery. Then will the Lord appear to his people, as He did to the typical Jew on the road to Damascus. "Then shall the Lord go forth, and fight against those nations, as when He fought in the day of battle." "Behold," says John, referring to the same event, "He cometh with clouds, and every eye shall see Him, and they which pierced Him, and all the tribes of the earth shall mourn over Him." "In that day," to quote Ezekiel's vivid and striking imaginery, "saith the Lord, when Gog shall come against the land of Israel, my fury shall come up into my nostrils. And I will plead against him with pestilence and with blood; and I will rain upon him, and upon his hordes, and upon the many peoples that are with him, an overflowing shower, and great hail-stones, fire, and brimstone. And I will magnify Myself, and sanctify Myself, and I will make Myself known in the eyes of many nations."

It is impossible to doubt that, at that time, there will be a literal appearance of the rejected Saviour. Where his feet often stood in the days of his flesh, they shall stand again. "His feet shall stand in that day upon the Mount of Olives, which is before Jerusalem on the East. The Lord my God shall come, and all the holy ones with Thee." In other words, there shall be a glorious and literal fulfilment of the reassuring words of the two men, who, clad in white and glistening raiment, stood beside the apostles on Olivet.

H

"Ye men of Galilee, why stand ye looking into heaven ? This Jesus, which was received up from you into heaven, shall so come in like manner as ye beheld Him going into heaven" (Acts i. 11). "And it shall be said in that day, Lo, this is our God; we have waited for Him, and He will save us: this is the Lord; we have waited for Him, we will be glad and rejoice in his salvation. For in this mountain shall the hand of the Lord rest, and Moab shall be trodden down in his place, even as straw is trodden down in the water of the dunghill" (Isa. xxv. 9, 10).

It was when his brethren were in their greatest straits that Joseph made himself known unto them; and when the Jews are in their dire extremity, they will cry aloud for help and deliverance from Him whom they rejected. That memorable scene in the ancient land of the pyramids will be reproduced in all its pathos, when the long-rejected Brother shall say to his own brethren after the flesh, "I am Jesus, your Brother, whom ye sold unto Pilate: and now be not grieved, nor angry with yourself, that ye delivered Me up to be crucified; for God did send Me before you to preserve a remnant in the earth, and to save you alive by a great deliverance" (see Gen. xlv. 1-15).

When this final reconciliation shall have taken place; when the mutual blessings and embracings have effaced the memory of the bitter past; when the chosen people shall have recognised their great Deliverer—He will set Himself to deliver them. It may be that they will recognise Him in the act of their deliverance. The cleaving mountain shall make a way of escape, as of old time the cleaving sea. On that memorable day—"one day, which is known unto the Lord, not day, and not night"; when the cold and frost (verse 6, R.V., *marg.*) shall mingle with the throes of earthquake (verse 5); when the sun shall be turned into darkness and the moon into blood; when atmospheric and cosmical convulsions, accompanying the crisis, give evidence of its momentous character, as the pangs of the travail-hour in which the new age is being born—God will destroy the face of the covering that is cast over all peoples, and the vail that is spread over all nations. He will swallow up death in victory, and the Lord God will wipe away tears from off all faces; and the reproach of his people shall He take away from off all the earth; for the Lord hath spoken it. How touching and significant are the prophet's words: "It shall come to pass, that at evening time it shall be light." The day of Israel's history has been long and stormy. For the most part, heavy storm-clouds have brooded over her national life, emitting from age to age thunder and deluges of rain; but already there is a rim of light on the horizon, and this is destined to grow until it dispossesses the brooding darkness. The sun shall yet break out and bathe the whole landscape with warm and glowing radiance. "At evening time it shall be light."

Whether we shall live to see that evening we cannot tell. But during these latter years, many signs have been giving evidence that we are approaching one of those epoch-making moments in the history of our race which may be called the hinges of the ages. The despair which is settling down on some of the noblest spirits; the excessive devotion to pleasure which engrosses the light and vain; the descent of empire from the gold of imperial autocracy to the iron and clay of the rule of the peoples; the lawless disregard of family ties and sacred institutions; the hatred bitter of the Jewish people, known as anti-Semitism, which, like a contagious fever, has befallen most of the European nations; the interesting movements among the Jews themselves, that known as Zionism, that identified with the name of Rabinovitch in South Russia, and those which are attempting the recolonization of the land of their fathers—all these announce the near approach of the fulfilment of these words. It seems, as we study contemporary history, that, in all likelihood, we are watching the first stages of scenes destined to culminate in the public reconciliation of the Jews with their Messiah.

The calculations of the most careful students of prophecy also indicate that we are approaching the time at which the times of the Gentiles run out, and at which the chosen people must be restored to their national prerogative and reinstated as God's representatives before the world. "Now from the fig-tree learn her parable. When her branch is now become tender, and putteth forth its leaves, ye know that the summer is nigh; even so ye also, when ye see all these things, know ye that He is nigh, even at the doors. Watch therefore: for ye know not what hour your Lord doth come."

Apparently the land of the Jews is destined to pass through considerable changes, dating from the time of the Lord's interposition on their behalf. The issue of living waters east and west; the depression of the surrounding country to the level of the Arabah, from Gibeah of Saul on the north to Rimmon on the south; the elevation of Jerusalem, as though to a level plateau; and the removal of the curse— are, of course, capable of metaphorical and figurative treatment: but there is no precise reason for doubting that the volcanic action, which is so clearly referred to in the fifth verse, will produce great modifications of the present landscape.

That the Jews shall be entirely victorious in that last great struggle is abundantly enforced. We learn from Ezekiel's visions of the same event that they that dwell in the cities of Israel shall go forth to make fires of the weapons of their foes, to burn them, so that they shall have no need to gather the wood of the forest for fuel; and that men will have to be set apart for the work of burying the multitudes of the dead. Here, too, we are told that when Judah fights *at* Jerusalem (not *against*, see R.V., *marg.*), the Lord shall smite the opposing hosts with a great plague, before which they shall be consumed; and that there shall be vast spoils of gold and silver, and apparel in great abundance.

This, surely, is the scene which the beloved apostle depicts in marvellous phraseology, thrilling with the splendour of his rich and glowing eloquence:

"I saw the heaven opened; and behold, a white horse, and He that sat thereon, called Faithful and True; and in righteousness He doth judge and make war. And his eyes are a flame of fire, and upon his head are many diadems; and He hath a name written, which no one knoweth but He Himself. And He is arrayed in a garment sprinkled with blood; and his name is called The Word of God. And the armies which are in heaven followed him upon white horses, clothed in fine linen, white and pure. And out of his mouth proceedeth a sharp sword, that with it He should smite the nations: and He shall rule them with a rod of iron: and He treadeth the winepress of the fierceness of the wrath of Almighty God. And He hath on his garment and on his thigh a name written—KING OF KINGS, AND LORD OF LORDS."

"And I saw an angel standing in the sun; and he cried with a loud voice, saying to all the birds that fly in mid-heaven, Come and be gathered together unto the great supper of God; that ye may eat the flesh of kings, and the flesh of captains, and the flesh of mighty men, and the flesh of horses and of them that sit thereon, and the flesh of all men, both free and bond, and small and great" (REV. xix. 11–18, R.V.).

So all Israel shall be saved. The envy also of Ephraim shall depart; Ephraim shall not envy Judah, and Judah shall not vex Ephraim. The mountain of the Lord's house shall be established in the top of the mountains, and all nations shall flow unto it. The holy city shall arise and shine, because her light is come, and the glory of the Lord is risen upon her; and all the glowing words of Isaiah's sixtieth chapter shall be gloriously fulfilled.

Behold the Lord, by many a prophet, and especially by his servant Zechariah, has proclaimed to the end of the earth: "Say ye to the daughter of Zion, Behold, thy salvation cometh!"

XV

THE MILLENNIAL AGE, AND THIS
(ZECHARIAH xiv. 16)

THE Feast of Tabernacles was one of the brightest and
gladdest of all the Hebrew Festivals. It commemorated the
wanderings of the children of Israel in the wilderness, when
they dwelt in booths. "Ye shall dwell in booths seven days,"
ran the ancient words of prescription; "all that are homeborn
in Israel shall dwell in booths, that your generations may
know that I made the children of Israel to dwell in booths,
when I brought them out of the land of Egypt" (Lev. xxiii.
39, &c.).

The time fixed for its celebration was after the harvest
was gathered in. "On the fifteenth day of the seventh month,
when ye have gathered in the fruits of the land, ye shall keep
the feast of the Lord seven days; on the first day shall be a
solemn rest, and on the eighth day shall be a solemn rest."
But the *rest* of that first day was consistent with the gathering
of branches of palm trees, boughs of thick trees, and willows
of the brook. What a joyful conjunction! The labours of
the year were over, the corn was in the barns, the wine and
oil were safely stored, the fields were resting in the mellow
sunshine, recuperating after their toils. From all parts of the
land the people gathered to the city of their fathers, whose
grim and ancient palaces and fortresses were festooned with
greenery, the roofs covered with bowers, and all the open
spaces packed close with leafy tabernacles. "The people
made themselves booths, every one upon the roof of his
house, and in their courts, and in the courts of the house of

God, and in the broad place of the water-gate, and in the broad place of the gate of Ephraim" (Neh. viii. 16).

To the quickened eye of the prophet, scenes were to take place again, similar to those recorded in the books of Ezra and Nehemiah (Ezra iii. 4; Neh. viii. 16); only in the glad days he anticipated there would gather not Jews alone, acknowledging the Divine King, but representatives of the nations of the world, gathered out of every land, and speaking in every tongue. "It shall come to pass, that every one that is left of all the nations which came against Jerusalem, shall go up from year to year to worship the King, the Lord of Hosts, and to keep the feast of Tabernacles." It is not requisite to believe that the literal feasts of the old covenant shall be restored; but that the gladness, the restfulness, the festal array, which pervaded the city at that time of the year, in the olden days, shall characterise the religious life of the world, the focus of which will be "the beloved city."

The fair vision that closes the vista of the glade of time to the Hebrew prophets, was always the rehabilitation of Jerusalem as the religious metropolis of the world. It was so once, when the Queen of Sheba led the devout enquirers of many lands to hear the wisdom of Solomon. It was so when at the day of Pentecost, its streets were filled with the Babel of languages from all the world, and men of different garb, complexion, and religion, poured through the tortuous streets. Spiritually, it has been so since, for more eyes have turned to Jerusalem than to Rome, and as the religion of Jesus has spread, the whole trend of religious thought has been towards the city where Christianity was born and cradled, and which is the type of the Jerusalem which is above, and is the mother of us all. But such conceptions will not satisfy the rich predictions of holy men, who spake as they were borne along by the Holy Ghost. The multitude of camels shall bring the pilgrims of the East, as the ships of Tarshish the children of the West. Through the wide-open gates the streams of worshippers shall pour into the city, bringing the wealth of the nations. Instead of being forsaken and hated, so that no man passed through, she shall become an eternal excellency, the joy of many generations.

Even in those halcyon days when righteousness shall begin to cover the earth—as waters the sea—when tidal waves of salvation shall sweep over the nations, some will be recalcitrant. The true conception of the Millennium does not imply that every single soul will be regenerate; but that the preponderating influences of the world shall be in favour of whatsoever things are just, pure, lovely, and of good report. As now the heavenlies are filled with the evil spirits, who rule the darkness of this world, so then they shall be filled with Christ and his saints, who shall rule the cities and continents in the direction of righteousness, temperance, and peace. But even under these favourable circumstances, the evil of the human heart will break out into obstinate rebellion, and some will refuse to submit to Israel's God. "And it shall be, that whoso of all the families of the earth goeth not up to Jerusalem to worship the King, the Lord of Hosts, upon them there shall be no rain. And if the family of Egypt go not up, and come not, ... there shall be the plague."

This adaptation of punishment to the circumstances of the lands which are the objects of Divine chastisement is very significant. Clearly it would be no punishment to the land of Egypt for rain to be withheld, as her prolific harvests depend on her mighty river. But she shall not therefore escape judgment; but for her there shall be the stroke of the plague. God leaves no sin unchastised; but He knows how to lay his hand on the spot where we are most vulnerable. There He touches us, and thus we are brought most swiftly to repentance. We cry, "Ah, if it had been anything but that, I could have borne it; but that was my Benjamin, my Rachel, the apple of my eye, the one sensitive spot where I am capable of the intensest suffering."

At this juncture a shaft of light breaks over the coming age, which stands revealed in all its beauties of holiness. We all know that the High Priest wore on his forehead a golden plate, on which the sacred words, HOLINESS TO THE LORD, were engraved. It was always on his mitre, held there by its lace of blue, that the people of Israel might be accepted before the Lord (Exod. xxviii. 36–38). But here the prophet sees that same inscription on the bells of the horses, and the common vessels of household use. "In that day shall there be upon the bells of the horses, HOLINESS UNTO THE LORD; and the pots in the Lord's house shall be like the bowls before the altar. Yea, every pot in Jerusalem and Judah shall be Holiness unto the Lord of Hosts."

Holiness stands for three things: Separation from sin and unbecomingness; devotion to the service of God; and that growing likeness to Him which is the necessary consequence of receiving Him as an Almighty Tenant of the heart. For holiness can never be an inherent and personal attribute; it must always be ours in proportion as we are God-possessed and God-filled. They are holiest who have most of God. It is a remarkably vivid portrayal of the distinction between Judaism and Christianity, that the word, which of all others characterised the exclusiveness and limitations of the old law, should be here appropriated to the most ordinary and commonplace of domesticities.

We have here, first, the abolition of the distinction between sacred and secular. Some people resemble ships, which are built in water-tight compartments; all their religion is kept carefully apart from the ordinary interests and pursuits of their existence. For instance, they go religiously to their place of worship on Sunday, but would be almost horrified if you were to mention the name of God in their drawing-room, or at the dining-table. They might even look at their guest reprovingly, as much as to say, There is a place and a time for everything, but not here or now. With such, Holiness to the Lord is well enough for the high priest and for the sanctuary; but it has no place on the bells of the horses, or the vessels of household use. Certainly the ostler in the stable, or the domestic servant about her duties, would have no right to use so reverend a designation.

But surely this rigid separation between duties as sacred and duties as secular, between clean and unclean, between holy and common, cannot be justified in the face of the teachings of the New Testament, which bid us do all, even eating and drinking, in the name of the Lord Jesus, and for the glory of God (1 Cor. x. 31; Col. iii. 17).

Besides, consider the genius and inner heart of Christianity. (1) *It brings us into the possession of a new life.* We are Christians, not because we avow a certain creed, or conform to certain outward exercises; but because we have received the life, the Eternal Life, which was with the Father, and was manifested unto us in Jesus. And is it possible to restrict the manifestations of life? Can a flower weave its petals and exhale its fragrance to order? Can the young things of the woodlands and meadows be thus to-day and something else to-morrow? Can a child observe days and times in its laughter, its tears, its appetite? Is not God's life always the same in its abundant and infinite variety? So surely the life of God in the soul should, and must, express itself in all the outgoings of our existence—in speech, act, movement—equally on the six days as the one day; as much in the kitchen, or the shop, as the church. If you are possessed by the life of the Holy One, it will as certainly appear as the idiosyncrasy of your character, which underlies, moulds, and fashions your every gesture.

(2) Moreover, *Christianity is Consecration to Christ.* It may be questioned if we have a right to call ourselves Christians unless we regard Him as our Judge, our Lawgiver, and our King, and are deliberately obeying and serving Him. But if we are going to reserve our religion to

certain days, places, and actions, we necessarily exclude Him from all that is not contained within the fences we erect. If it be measured by days, we exclude from the government, and therefore the peace, of Christ, at least six-sevenths of our time. Does the owner of a slave expect *his* ownership to be curtailed and narrowed after this fashion? Would he consider that he was receiving the value of his purchase-money, which he had paid down for the exclusive and unceasing rights of proprietorship? And what right have we to suppose that our Master Christ will be satisfied with an arrangement which asks Him to accept a part for the whole a composition for the entire debt?

(3) Then, also, *the needs of the world demand an entire and unbroken religious life.* The world does not see us in our religious exercises, whether in our private retirement or our public worship. It has no idea, therefore, of the anguish of our penitence, the earnestness of our desires for a righteous and noble life, the persistency of our endeavours. And if we do not give evidence of our religion in our dealings with matters that the men of the world understand, they will naturally and rightly consider that religion is an unpractical dream, the child of superstition and emotion. We need to witness to the world, where its paths intersect ours, and in regard to matters it can appreciate. If we are found to be more patient, truthful, honest, than other men; if our integrity can only be accounted for by causes beyond our ken —then the children of this age will be prepared to acknowledge that we have come into contact with sources of life and strength, which are clearly realities, but of which they know nothing.

For these reasons, we should refuse to maintain the false distinction between things that are sacred and those that are secular. There are right and wrong things in the world. The wrong ones are, of course, to be fenced out of our lives; but all right ones are sacred. Everything that may be done at all, may be done to Christ, and in being done to Him, is rendered holy. The ostler with his horses, the servant with the vessels of her household service, the clerk with his pen, the mechanic with his tool, the guide with his alpenstock, the artist with his camera, may realize that those mystic words are graven on his forehead, and in the instrument of his toil. And each one of us, on entering the workshop of his life, may feel that he is serving God there as much as if he were entering the shrine of some holy temple, and were called to minister at God's altar. The pots and vessels may be looked on as though they were the vessels in which the victims' blood was collected as it flowed from the sacrificial knife.

II. THERE MAY BE THE INCLUSION OF MANY THINGS WHICH ONCE SEEMED SECULAR, IF WE CAN CONSECRATE THEM TO CHRIST.—The Jews were forbidden to own horses. With a tear in his voice, the sacred chronicler records it as a sign of Solomon's degeneracy that he brought horses up out of Egypt. Horses were associated with the pride and pomp of kings, and savoured of the arm of flesh, therefore they were prohibited. "Some trust in chariots," said the psalmist, "and some in horses; but we will remember the name of the Lord our God." But here they are specially accepted and acknowledged. They are included in the prophet's anticipation of the blessed future. But notice, HOLINESS TO THE LORD is now engraven upon the bells that make sweet music as they move.

What a graphic and significant manner of teaching one of the profoundest lessons !

Judaism, with its special days, places, and men, had its part in the religious training of the race. It was the Kindergarten of human childhood; but when we become men, we put away childish things. Probably every life, in its earliest stages, must be fenced and partitioned off from things which, however innocent in themselves, are prejudicial to its development. It was impossible for God to teach men what holiness meant, save by this process of prohibition, of separation, and of setting apart. But, when the lesson was fully learnt, the Levitical code was abolished, and Jesus came, saying, "It was said to them of old time; . . . but *I* say unto you." The horses which might not be used, came to be as much in vogue as the bowls of the altar or the household vessels, and to bear upon their harness the significant sentence that gleamed aforetime on the forehead of Aaron and his sons.

In the middle ages, saintly souls dreaded to enter the sacred relationships of home, and thought that the babble and prattle of babes, and the love of wife, were inimical to their highest interests. But they sadly misread Christ's meaning; they forgot that He sat at Cana's feast; they failed to understand that nothing included in God's original creation could be common and unclean. It is a more excellent and Christ-like way to follow the dictates of nature and of the heart, only with the resolve and purpose that human love should be a chalice full of the Eternal and the Divine, and that on the most intimate relationships of life, "Holiness to the Lord" should be inscribed.

So with recreation. It is not wrong to unbend the bow in manly games, that develop the sinews and expand the lungs, or to join in the pastimes of your age and companions, so long as you can write on bat and football, on tennis racquet and piano, on oar and paddle, on skate or sleigh, the words of the High Priest's frontal, HOLINESS TO THE LORD. Whatever you cannot pray over, refuse to touch. Whatever you can make a matter of prayer and consecration is legitimate. Every thing is good, and not to be refused, which can be received with thanksgiving; for it is sanctified by the Word of God and prayer.

The same rule applies to the enjoyment of nature, of art, of music, of beautiful objects, whether sculptured or carved, photographed or painted. True holiness does not consist in bare walls, and hard seats, and a dingy environment; but in all that resembles God's work in nature, which is exquisitely beautiful, whether it be the creepers that change to crimson in the autumn, or the enamelling of the rocks, or the tessellated floors of the woodlands, or the silver features of the stars.

Take the horses into the economy of your life; only see to it that the memory of "Holiness to the Lord" recurs to you at every movement of their arching necks.

Let us take note that there must be an elevation of all life to the level of our sacred and religious moments. It would be, of course, possible to obliterate the distinction between sacred and secular by treating all as secular; but this would be a desecration of our life indeed. The process is not one of levelling-down, but of levelling-up. The Lord's house must be established "on the top of the mountains," and all nations are to flow to it. It is not that the priest is to take off his sacred emblem when he enters the sanctuary; but that he is to put it on when he goes to the stable to mount his horse. It is not that the bowls of the altar are to be ejected from their sacred office there; but that common vessels— "every pot in Jerusalem and Judah"—is to be treated with equal regard. It is not that the sanctuary is to be abolished; but that all other places are to become oratories for prayer and shrines for holy service. It is thus that we are to be able to dwell in the house of the Lord all the days of our life.

We cannot make all time sacred unless we set apart special hours and days for God. We cannot carry the spirit of pure and undefiled religion among our fellows, unless we often enter into our closet and shut the door, and pray unto our Father, who is in secret. We cannot do all tasks to the glory of God, unless we have mountains of transfiguring prayer. We cannot read all books and papers in a religious spirit, unless we are loving and systematic Bible-students. We cannot use ordinary vessels as though they were the bowls of the altar, unless we handle the bowls of that altar, which is in the possession of all holy souls who do not serve the tabernacle. "Wherefore, forsake not the assembling of yourselves, as the manner of some is"; . . . and, "Remember the Sabbath-day to keep it holy."

So many bells ring out in our lives. The morning wakening bell, and the school-bell; the work-bell for the mechanic, and the shop-bell for the assistant; the visitors' bell on one side of the door, and the tradesmen's on the other; the wedding bells with their merry peal, and the funeral bells with their sorrowful monotone; the bicyclist's bell warning the foot-passenger on to the pavement, and the bells on the sleigh-horses, as they draw the vehicle over the frozen snow. To many of these, in times past, we have given a lethargic, listless, and indolent response; we have resented their intrusion on our slumbers and plans; we have chafed against their peremptory summons. But enough of this. Henceforth, let us hear in their clangour or chime the call of God to the tasks to which He summons us; let us obey with alacrity, looking to Him for grace and strength to do whatever He would have us do, and realizing that on each the inscription of Aaron's frontal-piece is engraven,

"HOLINESS UNTO THE LORD."